W.A. Begole's Tin Shop in 1878

Forgotten by most San Diego histories, the author discovered her 19th century "Cousin Gus Begole" quite by accident in 2009 while reading Richard Pourade's well-known History of San Diego. There in Pourade's volume four was her mother's rare Huguenot surname — glamorously attached to a member of an 1875 sheriff's posse.

This story is the product of the author's search for W.A. Begole's place in her family history and in the history of San Diego, and of her exhilarating discoveries along the way of a generation of intrepid 19th century cousins, grandsons (and granddaughters) of the American Revolution, who helped build the American West.

# SAN DIEGO CITY FATHER WILLIAM AUGUSTUS BEGOLE

## ⋄ Story of a Workhorse Pioneer ⋄

# SAN DIEGO CITY FATHER WILLIAM AUGUSTUS BEGOLE

## ⟡ Story of a Workhorse Pioneer ⟡

# Lael Montgomery

Copyright ® 2017 by Lael Montgomery.
All rights reserved. The use of any part of this publication, reproduced, transmitted in any form or by any means, electronic, mechanical, photocopying, recording or otherwise stored in a retrieval system, without the prior consent of the publisher is an infringement of the copyright law.

Patricia Harriman, FinalEyes, copy editor
Jim Diggins, JD Indexing Services, indexer
Marcy Llamas Senese, FinalEyes, proofreader
Melany Runyan, "LM" logo designer
David Moratto, cover and interior designer
Published in the United States by Lael Montgomery,
Thundernut Farm, 13678 McNally Road,
Valley Center, California 92082

Includes bibliographic references and index.

First edition
Printed in the U.S.A.

ISBN: 978-0-9984405-1-4

*This story about William Augustus Begole's nineteenth-century life is dedicated to my husband, Jonathan Vick, a volunteer champion of back country roads, parks, walking trails and other amenities in our town, and to generations of community-makers whose contributions have escaped written history. Thank you all for your enduring gifts to our world. Thank you, Jon, for your steadfast dedication to every community to which you belong and most especially for your encouragement of this and so many other projects of mine and others.*

# The 2016 Restoration of City Father Begole's "Little Slogan"

In the San Diego Union on July 13, 1876, was the following report of the city's American Independence Day celebration: "At 5 o'clock (on the morning of July 4, 1876) the Silver Cornet band announced the dawn of the centennial Fourth by a medley of National airs from the cupola of the Horton House, while the sharp voiced little gun which **City Father Begole** has recently had made, boomed away briskly with a National salute. Everybody was soon stirring and for the next two hours there was a carnival of noise—cannon, small arms and every description of firecracker and Chinese bomb."[1]

*"Little Slogan" on its caisson in Horton Plaza, around 1930*

Known as "Little Slogan," San Diego's party cannon was ordered in 1876 by City Trustee President William Augustus Begole. Begole said in a San Diego Union article in 1892 that it was purchased "entirely by Republicans."[2] For years, between parades and city celebrations, the cannon sat on its caisson in Horton Plaza. Sometime after this photograph was taken, around 1930, the cannon disappeared. After spending much of the 20th century as a yard ornament at the Zink family's residence in San Diego, the long-lost cannon was recovered in 2013 by Save Our Heritage Organisation. The cannon was restored in 2016 to its former glory by SOHO, underwritten by the author and other members of the Begole Family.

*San Diego City Father William Augustus Begole
(1826–1901)*

# Contents

## Preface

How I Discovered William Augustus Begole . . . . . . . . . . xvii
The Family Puzzle . . . . . . . . . . . . . . . . . . . . . . . . xviii
The California Puzzle . . . . . . . . . . . . . . . . . . . . . . . xix
Prominent in Primary Historical Sources . . . . . . . . . . . . xxi
Crossed the Plains with the Donner Party . . . . . . . . . . . xxiii

## Chapter One

Nevada County to San Diego in 1869 . . . . . . . . . . . . . . . 1

## Chapter Two

1826: Beginnings — Genesee County, New York . . . . . . . . . 7
1840: Death of W. A.'s Mother and His Father's Remarriage . . 11

## Chapter Three

1846–49: Nevada County, California . . . . . . . . . . . . . . 13
1860s: Red Dog Ventures Sweet and Sour . . . . . . . . . . . 19
1866: Red Dog Destroyed by Fire, W. A. Begole Rebuilds . . . 21
1867–68: Red Dog Succumbs to Deluge and Exhausted Mining . . 24

## Chapter Four

1869: New Beginning in San Diego . . . . . . . . . . . . . . . 27
1870s: Sliding into the "News Boys" Network . . . . . . . . . 28
The Brotherhood of Freemasonry . . . . . . . . . . . . . . . . 29
Public Service and Private Enterprise . . . . . . . . . . . . . 33

## Chapter Five

*Between Booms: Mid 1870s to the Early 1880s* . . . . . . . . . . 37
*529 Fifth Street: W. A.'s "Home Office"* . . . . . . . . . . . . 41
*The Republican Advantage* . . . . . . . . . . . . . . . . . . . 42
*1881, Marriage. 1882, Divorce* . . . . . . . . . . . . . . . . . 46

## Chapter Six

*Early 1880s: Run-Up to San Diego's Late '80s Boom-a-Rama* . . . 51
*Cousin Josiah William Begole Elected Michigan Governor* . . . . 52
*1885: Through Train from San Diego to the Continent* . . . . . 54

## Chapter Seven

*1886: W. A.'s Life Shift at 60* . . . . . . . . . . . . . . . . 57
*1888: W. A. Begole and the New City Charter Elections* . . . . 59
*The New Regime: Stewardship and Non-Partisanship* . . . . . . . 61

## Chapter Eight

*1890s: W. A.'s Last Decade* . . . . . . . . . . . . . . . . . . 65

Appreciations and Acknowledgements . . . . . . . . . . . . . . . 73
Endnotes . . . . . . . . . . . . . . . . . . . . . . . . . . . . 75
Bibliography . . . . . . . . . . . . . . . . . . . . . . . . . . 87
Index . . . . . . . . . . . . . . . . . . . . . . . . . . . . . 101
Photograph, Illustration, and Map Credits . . . . . . . . . . . 119
About the Author . . . . . . . . . . . . . . . . . . . . . . . 123

## Photographs, Illustrations, and Maps

"Little Slogan" the 1876 Party Cannon . . . . . . . . . . . . . . . . . . vii
William Augustus Begole . . . . . . . . . . . . . . . . . . . . . . . . . . ix
W. A. Begole's Obituary, San Francisco Call, 1901 . . . . . . . . . xxiii
S.S. Senator at Horton's Wharf . . . . . . . . . . . . . . . . . . . . . . . 1
5th Street Looking North from K Street, 1869–1870 . . . . . . . . 2
W. A. Begole's Tin Shop at 529 Fifth, in 1874 . . . . . . . . . . . . . 2
Last Rail Spike Ceremony, 1869 . . . . . . . . . . . . . . . . . . . . . . 3
Map of Nevada County Gold Mining Towns . . . . . . . . . . . . . 14
Map of the Historic Town of Red Dog, CA . . . . . . . . . . . . . . 15
W. A. Begole's Advertisement in Beans Magazine, 1867 . . . . . . 23
Boston Hydraulic Gold Mine, Red Dog, 1879 . . . . . . . . . . . . 25
W. A. Begole's Advertisement in the San Diego Bulletin, 1870 . . . 29
W. A. Begole's Application to San Diego Lodge No. 35 . . . . . . 30
W. A. Begole's Masonic Officers' Jewels . . . . . . . . . . . . . . . . 32
Gaskill's Store in Campo, 1880's . . . . . . . . . . . . . . . . . . . . . 34
W. A. Begole's Tin Trunk for San Diego Lodge No. 35 . . . . . . 38
W. A. Begole's 1876 Invoice to San Diego Lodge No. 35 . . . . . 39
W. A. Begole's Tin Shop, 529 Fifth Street, 1878 and 2012 . . . 42–43
Masonic Building at 6th and H Streets . . . . . . . . . . . . . . . . . 51
Florence Hotel . . . . . . . . . . . . . . . . . . . . . . . . . . . . . . . . . 53
First National Bank . . . . . . . . . . . . . . . . . . . . . . . . . . . . . 53
Fifth Street Looking South from Broadway in 1888 . . . . . . . . 59
San Diego Lodge No. 35 Meeting Notice, March 1900 . . . . . . 67
Mason's Notices of W. A. Begole's Death, 1901 . . . . . . . . . . . 70
W. A. Begole's Gravestone at Mount Hope Cemetery . . . . . . . 70
Fifth Street, San Diego, Pictured Across Time . . . . . . . . . . . . 71

*" ... life is sad  
if you haven't lived it  
for a dream ... "*  
—Chilean Lullaby

# PREFACE

*How I Discovered that San Diego City Father
William Augustus Begole Is a First Cousin
and Came to Write His Story*

While reading Richard Pourade's multivolume *History of San Diego* several years ago, I was stunned and intrigued to see that a member of a celebrated 1875 San Diego posse shared my mother's rare Huguenot surname "Begole."[3] My maternal grandparents, Michigander transplants to Boston, where I grew up, had never mentioned a San Diego pioneer in the family. This tidbit haunted my imagination until I joined Ancestry, GenealogyBank, Fold 3, and a bunch of other genealogical sources and started riffling through family records, census records, local histories, and (at last!) historical newspapers in an effort to learn this fellow's place in my mother's family tree and, as it turns out, California history.

Surprisingly, except for Pourade's brief mention, William Augustus Begole has been ignored by formal histories despite his prominence in business, civic, and fraternal affairs in Northern and Southern California during the second half of the nineteenth century. W. A.'s extensive activities as a miner, investor, businessman, and civic leader in Little York Township (Red Dog, You Bet, Chalk Bluff) in Nevada County, California, and later in the new city of San Diego, are revealed through primary sources: historical newspapers, city government rosters, court records, election records, and organization rosters.

Five years and hundreds of documents later (there are more than 500 citations on GenealogyBank alone), I understand how William Augustus Begole (1826–1901) fits into my family history and how his life story fits into the history of California. From the factual records, we can piece together activities, events, and turning points in W. A. Begole's life. Unfortunately, his diary, which he bequeathed to San Diego Lodge No. 35 in 1901, disappeared from the Lodge archives in the 1920s. No other personal communications except his last will and testament have survived. We might imagine a bit about his character from a scattering of W. A.'s experiences, actions, and alliances. But his own thoughts and feelings, and the impressions he made on his contemporaries, we will never know.

## *The Family Puzzle*

William Augustus Begole is my first cousin, four times removed. His father was the brother of my third great-grandfather, the generation born after the American Revolution and who served in the War of 1812. W. A. is also cousin to a cluster of other nineteenth-century Begoles[4] who were intrepid, colorful, and notable settlers of the American West. He is also first cousin (also four times removed) to Robert "Bob" Begole for whom the Begole Archeological Center in Borrego Springs, California, is named. We cousins across four generations all descend from two Begole brothers who settled the Genesee Valley in New York around 1815 after serving in the War of 1812. Our common ancestors are their parents—people who settled in Maryland before the American Revolution and immigrated before 1810 to Upstate New York.

I know this now from family tracking and following hunches, mostly in the Federal Census, beginning in 1790 in Maryland—following not just my research subject but all members of all the Begole families in the area (called "cluster research"), and comparing this information with data gleaned from histories of the settlement of small towns in Upstate New York. My cousin by marriage, genealogist Ellen Gerwitz of Rochester, New York, skillfully led me on this rambling adventure, teaching me much about how to find, assemble, triangulate, and interpret information in census records. William Augustus Begole did not appear by name in any of these New York records. I was not entirely sure that we had assigned him to the right set of parents until

I compared sibling information from census records with death and cemetery records, and probate records in New York and in San Diego. Bingo! William Augustus Begole's 1895 will named his brothers and sisters and their children.

## The California Puzzle: W. A. Begole's Trail ~ Gold Country and San Diego

Cracking the California puzzle was tedious but much more straightforward. I could assemble a timeline from historical newspapers and other documents. GenealogyBank has more than 500 newspaper articles citing W. A. Begole and several hundred more citing other Begoles who were also roaming around the American West between 1840 and 1900. The Nevada County Historical Society and the San Diego History Center have a scattering of newspaper citations on microfiche and in court records from the 1850s that cite W. A. Begole. Historical property records in Nevada and San Diego Counties track his land purchases and sales from the 1850s. Additional government documents, such as precinct and election records, and bits of information from the archives of private, civic, and fraternal organizations helped complete the picture. By working back and forth across all these, I was able to piece together W. A.'s story and identify how W. A. and the others fit into the family story and into the larger nineteenth century histories of Nevada County and San Diego.

This is what I learned.

# ⊰ Prominent in Primary Historical Sources for Fifty ⊱ Years and in San Diego's Foundational Institutions

William Augustus Begole figures prominently in business, civic, and fraternal affairs for the fifty years after his arrival in California (in Nevada County in 1849/50 and in San Diego in 1869) until his death in September, 1901. Newspapers, election records, organization rosters, and legal and civic records reveal that W. A. Begole was a leader among the pioneer miners in Little York Township, a Justice of the Peace, owner-builder of the ditches from the Yuba River that enabled hydraulic mining, a delegate to American and Republican conventions, and a founding director of the fire department and the Mount Carmel Masonic Lodge.

In San Diego, W. A. served as one of five elected city trustees for five years, was trustee president for a year and a half, and a city alderman for two. He was also: an early investor in the San Diego-Yuma Turnpike; a San Diego Reading Room Association Trustee and member of the Board of Managers; Vice President of the Citizens Railroad Committee, Vice President of the Grant-Wilson Club; Chairman of the Republican County Committee and many times a convention delegate; and a Republican Club officer and member of the Finance Committee as well as a dedicated party leader and booster of Republican candidates, initiatives, and projects.

He was further a San Diego Library Trustee, a first and second Vice President of the San Diego Chamber of Commerce, a recording secretary of the San Diego Society of Natural History, and a Pacific Railroad investor. He was appointed many times an election judge and inspector for Ward 3 and to the County Grand Juror pool. He was elected in 1888 as one of the fifteen freemen who drafted the new San Diego City Charter, and in 1889, he was one of nine aldermen elected with Mayor Douglas Gunn to implement the new charter. As an alderman, he was appointed to draft the new tax levy, served on committees on Water and Fire, Public Buildings and Lighting, and Police and

Health and Morals and was appointed to the Board of Equalization. During the struggle in the late 1890s between municipal and private ownership of water infrastructure and service, W. A. Begole was rallied out of retirement to be a vice president of the Municipal Ownership Club.

A dedicated long-term member, six-term master, and high priest, W. A. Begole served San Diego Masonic Lodge No. 35, Royal Arch Masons No. 61, and San Diego Commandery No. 25 Knights Templar in innumerable ways and also presided over the Masonic Building Association for many years.

William Augustus Begole was also a tinsmith; he built the tin roofs on the Florence Hotel and the National and Commercial Banks as well as on a number of private homes in the late 1870s and early 1880s. Listing his occupation as "capitalist" in the 1890 US Census, he invested in gold mines in Julian, Pine Valley, and the Temecula areas, and to some extent also in real estate, the railroad, and some public works projects.

## CROSSED THE PLAINS WITH DONNER PARTY

### W. A. Begole, a Pioneer of the Golden West, Passes Away in San Diego.

SAN DIEGO, Sept. 2.—W. A. Begole, one of the oldest residents of San Diego and a pioneer of California, died last evening of neuralgia of the heart. He came to this coast in 1849 as a member of the Donner party. He spent several years in the central part of the State and came to San Diego thirty-three years ago. He was for years the leading hardware merchant and plumber of the city, but retired almost a decade ago.

Mr. Begole was prominent in Masonic circles and was master of San Diego Lodge No. 35 from 1871 to 1875 and again in 1885. He left no family and no relatives except a brother, ex-Governor Begole of Michigan.

The funeral to-morrow forenoon will be in charge of the Masons and will call together the largest gathering of the order that has been seen in San Diego in years.

W. A. Begole's obituary in the *San Francisco Call*[5] refers incorrectly to the year 1849 for the Donner tragedy. The Donner-Reed prairie crossing ended at Donner Lake near Truckee in 1846. Because the origin of this conflicting information is unknown, we are left to wonder whether W. A. travelled in 1846 with the Donner family and the date in the newspaper was an editorial error, or whether he travelled in 1849 and the Donner detail was maybe "misremembered" by W. A. himself or by someone else. Another biographical detail that is misreported in some sources is W. A.'s relationship to Michigan Governor Josiah William Begole. They were first cousins, not brothers.

# CHAPTER ONE

### Nevada County to San Diego in 1869

**W**ILLIAM AUGUSTUS BEGOLE arrived in San Diego from San Francisco on the sidewheel steamer *S.S. Senator* on September 24, 1869.[6] Known to historians as Black Friday, the day the US Gold Market collapsed, it was also the first day that the freight and passenger steamer the *S.S. Senator* would sail past its usual landing at Culverwell's Wharf in Old Town to tie up at Horton's Wharf. Just finished, the new wharf was closer to the new firms on Fifth Street in Alonzo E. Horton's "New Town" and closer to the future of San Diego than its past. The promise of gold and growth likely drew tinsmith, hardware dealer, miner, and "capitalist" W. A. Begole to the dry, dusty, sparsely populated outpost of San Diego in the 1870s.

*The S.S. Senator at Horton's Wharf at the base of Fifth Street, circa 1869*

When W. A. Begole sailed into San Diego in September of 1869, it was probably not his first visit. The month before, for $350 in gold coin, he had purchased a double lot on Fifth Street.[7] The fact that the seller was not New Town developer A. E. Horton but was Ole N. Lee shows that lots in the new subdivision known as "Horton's Addition" were already turning over and that the '70s land boom was underway.

*Fifth Street in San Diego looking north from K Street around 1869–1870*

*W. A. Begole's tin shop on the south side of the double lot on Fifth Street in 1874, next to Steiner & Klauber's market*

W. A. located his tin shop on the southern half of this property at 529 Fifth Street, between Market and Island. Six months later, in March of 1870, Begole speculated again in New Town real estate and purchased directly from A. E. Horton a lot on Sixth Street,[9] paying $1,000 in gold coin. The Sixth Street lot was adjacent to the corner lot at J Street but not the premium corner position. Nevertheless, W. A. paid 300% more than he'd paid just six months previously for the double lot on Fifth Street.

At the ceremony for the driving of the last spike at Promontory Summit, Utah, May 10, 1869.[8] Rumors of an RR link to San Diego excited the land boom years, 1867–1873

In 1869, W. A. Begole was forty-three years old. Before his move to San Diego, he had been settled in Nevada County gold country for about twenty years. We cannot know for certain his rationale for choosing San Diego for his home in 1869. However, events and circumstances around that time point to opportunities pulling him south, particularly the discovery of gold in the Wynola hills near Julian,[10] Horton's enterprising and widespread promotion of his vision for a "New Town" San Diego,[11] and frothy talk of rail service to link the natural port to the new trans-continental railroad and the rest of country.

The years 1868 and 1869 were boom years for San Diego. Plans for a new railroad were helping to fuel the interest. In May, 1868 General Thomas Sedgwick, surveyor and agent for John C. Fremont's Memphis, El Paso, and Pacific Railroad project published his report that named San Diego as the terminus for a planned transcontinental line. Soon both Old Town and New Town, or Horton's Addition as it was sometimes called, were booming. The prospect of the railroad brought hundreds of new settlers. By early 1870 New San Diego had a population of 2,301, with 915 residential and 69 business buildings.[12]

In addition to the "pull" of opportunity in San Diego was the "push" of cascading catastrophes in the 1860s with his mining enterprises in Little York Township—increasing consolidation in Nevada County of unprofitable small-scale mines by a few large, well-funded hydraulic operators combined with a series of man-made and natural disasters to make recovery there unpalatable. W. A.'s Little York stamp mill was destroyed by fire in 1861, as was the entire town of Red Dog, including his tin shop and theater. The fires were followed by record-setting floods that destroyed most of the town of Red Dog as well as the water works that enabled hydraulic mining in the area.

Like so many members of his generation, William Augustus Begole was no stranger to new beginnings or the pioneer life. He had grown up in the frontier of Upstate New York, and as a young man, had crossed the country from his birthplace in the Genesee Valley sometime in the late 1840s. His obituary says he "crossed the prairie with the Donner Party in 1849."[13] But, exactly when W. A. Begole travelled to California is uncertain because the Donner and Reed families left Independence, Missouri not in 1849 but in early May of 1846 with the much larger Russell-Boggs wagon train—63 wagons and 288 persons. Was W. A. Begole part of this group? Stewart[14] and others have written that the census of the Russell-Boggs wagon train was dynamic and that there is no reliable record of people who joined the train or dropped away. (Neither do we find confirmation of his arrival in California records, which were, of course, few and sketchy before statehood. There are no traces of W. A. Begole in California before 1850. Still, it is possible that this twenty-year-old single man travelled west with this group in 1846 around the start of the Mexican-American War and three years before the discovery of gold at Sutter Creek.)

Harvard historian Bernard DeVoto makes the point in his book, *The Year of Decision 1846*,[15] that 1846 was an especially significant turning point in America's destiny during which the notion of "manifest destiny"—the nation stretching from sea to sea—was realized through the United States' acquisition of Texas by annexation; of the Mexican territories of California, Nevada, Utah, Arizona, and New Mexico by conquest; and of Oregon by treaty with the British. Thousands of people loaded their belongings into wagons and trekked west.

Generational sociologists William Strauss and Neil Howe in their book, *Generations: The History of America's Future, 1584–2069*, call the generation born in the years between 1822 and 1842 the "Gilded Generation."[16] The young adulthoods of this cohort were frenetic years according to Strauss and Howe. They quote Mark Twain: "two-hundred thousand young men—not simpering, dainty, kid-gloved weaklings but stalwart, muscular dauntless young braves, brimful of push and energy—caught the California sudden-riches disease." The opportunity beckoning from the new frontier was likely good enough reason to "pull" a twenty-year-old toward the American West, especially a twenty-year-old like William Augustus Begole who may also have been "pushed" by family circumstances to pursue a new life on his own several thousand miles from home.

# Chapter Two

## 1826: Beginnings — Genesee County, New York

**W**ILLIAM AUGUSTUS BEGOLE was born in the wilderness of Mount Morris, Genesee County, New York, in October, 1826 to Benjamin and Margaret Schull Begole. He was next to the youngest of six children born across sixteen years. He had two sisters, Elizabeth and Nancy, ten and eight years older, and three brothers, Joseph six years and Joshua two years older. Benjamin was five years younger. We see in this brood many of the family's favorite names: William, Augustus, Benjamin, Joshua, Elizabeth, and Nancy.

The oft-repeated family story is that the Begoles were descendants of French Huguenots who immigrated to Virginia before 1700 to avoid France's persecution of Protestants. Public records show William Augustus' grandfather, William Rivers Begole, was living in Frederick County, Maryland by the time of the American Revolution where he owned some land, engaged in farming, and served as a corporal in the patriot militia.[17] According to the Federal Censuses of 1790 and 1800, there were no slaves in the William Begole (Begold) household.[18]

Around 1805, William Rivers Begole moved his wife and six of their grown children, including William Augustus' father, Benjamin Franklin Begole, from Hagerstown to the fertile Genesee Valley. They were following their eldest son, Thomas Jefferson Begole (1776–1854), to his post as land agent at the Hermitage in Groveland, New York, for the Maryland Company owned by the abundantly landed and rich Fitzhugh and Carroll families. These Maryland neighbors had purchased thousands of acres in Western New York with another well-heeled and also slaveholding Marylander, Nathaniel Rochester. Though one of these adult Begole siblings kept moving west to Illinois, five of them married and raised their families in the Genesee Valley.[19]

W. A. Begole's father, Benjamin Franklin Begole (1786–1869), was born in Hagerstown three years after the American Revolution ended. His younger brother, another William Augustus Begole (1788–1862, and for whom the subject of this biography was named), was born two years later. Theirs was the generation that served in the War of 1812. Benjamin Begole and his brother William both served in Colonel Philetus Swift's Regiment of New York.[20] After the war, these two brothers both married and located in the village of Mount Morris, New York. Their parents and three other siblings settled and re-settled in nearby frontier outposts of Groveland, Dansville, Wayland, Avon, and Geneseo. Benjamin Franklin Begole married Margaret Shull, most likely a daughter of one of two Schull brothers who emigrated from Maryland to Dansville, New York. Benjamin's brother and W. A.'s uncle William Augustus married Eleanor Bowles, daughter of another relocated Maryland neighbor, Thomas Augustus Bowles. (Both these families were apparently crazy for the name Augustus.) Thomas Augustus Bowles had moved his family also from Hagerstown, Maryland to Wayland, New York in the early 1800s.[23]

This bare-bones genealogical history suggests that William Augustus Begole grew up in an extended and tightly knit family of at least sixteen children of the two Begole brothers in the sparsely populated wilds of Mount Morris, in Upstate New York, in the first quarter of the nineteenth century. The two families all played, worked, and attended the one-room school together and depended upon one another.

## ‹ THESE TWO BEGOLE BROTHERS, THEIR WIVES AND CHILDREN ›

*Benjamin Franklin Begole (1786–1869)
and Margaret Schull Begole (1794–1840)*[22]
◊ Six children ◊

Elizabeth (Betsey) (1816–1836) killed in a buggy accident in Mount Morris
Nancy (1818–1892) married Nathan Bills, remained in Mount Morris, NY
Joseph (1820–1876) stayed in Mount Morris, NY
Joshua (1824–1907) emigrated to Burlingame, KS
**William Augustus (1826–1901) emigrated to Red Dog and San Diego, CA**
Benjamin Bradley (1831–1876) emigrated to Chicago, IL

*William Augustus Begole (1788–1862)
and Eleanor Bowles Begole (1794–1871)*
◊ Ten children ◊

Josiah William (1815–1896) emigrated to Flint, MI, and became Governor of Michigan
Frederick Augustus (1817–1896) emigrated to Flint, MI
Thomas Benjamin Begole (1819–1915) emigrated to Flint, MI
Sarah Eleanor (1821–1915) married Hezekiah Brinkerhoff and emigrated to Ypsilanti, MI
Cornelia Jane (1823–1902) married Hiram Mills, emigrated to Detroit, MI
Myron H. (1825–1863) emigrated to Cedar, IA; killed in the Civil War
Philo M. Begole (1828–1896) emigrated to Cedar, IA, and then to Flint/Vienna, MI[23]
George William (1830–1831) stayed in Mount Morris, NY
Julia Begole (1832–1892) married Malcolm McLachlen, emigrated to Kansas City, MO
William Franklin (1836–1912) emigrated to Belleville, MI

Mount Morris during William's childhood was still a true frontier settlement. Purchased from the Seneca Indians by a white trader in the late 1790s and later by Robert Morris, financier of the American Revolution for whom the town is named, parcels from The Morris Reserve were sold to settlers. The Town of Mount Morris was separated from the town of Leicester in 1813.[24] W. A.'s father Benjamin Begole and his Uncle William Begole, after serving in the War of 1812,

> purchased a track of wild timberland ... about two miles from the site of the present village of Mount Morris, and in the midst of the forest erected a log cabin, the customary dwelling of the early settlers. There were neither railways or canals traversing the country at that time; and Rochester, the nearest marketing and milling point, thirty-six miles distant, was accessible by teams only, three days being consumed in making the round trip. For many years after [their] settlement deer, bears, wolves, and other wild animals roamed the forests and were often a terror to the inhabitants.[25]
>
> By 1813 Mount Morris had four frame and 22 log houses. Small stores, artisans' shops and grist and lumber mills were established in the early 1800s as Mount Morris developed into a self-supporting community. Early industries included wool carding, a grist mill, a distillery that used the wheat grown on the flats, and the making of cloth from hemp also grown on the flats ...[26]

While the Town of Mount Morris was established in 1818, the village was not incorporated until 1835[27] when W. A. was nine years old. Reminiscing in 1882 about those early days in a speech, W. A.'s cousin Governor Josiah Begole said,

> our dwellings were built of round logs just as they were found in the primeval forest. Occasionally a pioneer would build his residence by hewing the logs both outside and in, providing he was so fortunate as to have a little spare money that he had

earned before coming here. This was called "aristocratic" or "putting on the style." The fireplace was always ample, often extending more than half way across the house .... Some of us remember with pleasure the big backlog drawn to the door with oxen, and requiring the combined strength of the family to place in position; then a smaller log was placed on top, making a fire that imparted both light and warmth to the family group gathered about the hearth.[28]

## 1840: Death of W. A.'s Mother and His Father's Remarriage

W. A.'s mother died in July 1840, the year Charles Henry Dana published his romantic California tale, *Two Years Before the Mast*. W. A. was fourteen years old. His oldest sister, Elizabeth (Betsey), had been killed in a wagon accident four years earlier.[29] In May 1840, just two months before his mother's death, his sister Nancy had married Nathan Bills, a local fellow. Still living at home with their father were the four boys: Joseph (20), Joshua (16), W. A. (14), and Ben (9). The next March, only eight months after their mother's death, their father, Benjamin, remarried thirty-year-old Maria Ewart of Groveland.[30] Maria was only a few years older than W. A.'s sister Nancy, and the new marriage was also something of a convoluted family affair. W. A.'s new stepmother was also his cousin by marriage. (Maria's brother, Harvey Ewart, was married to W. A.'s first cousin Mathilde Begole, daughter of Benjamin's older brother, Thomas Begole,[31] the Groveland land agent.) Marriages of cousins were still quite frequent and ordinary in the nineteenth century

Ten years later, according to the 1850 Federal Census, none of Benjamin Begole's first family of children were living with their father and new stepmother. W. A.'s older brothers Joseph and Joshua were unmarried farmers, boarding in the Mount Morris household of a family that lived next door to their uncle William Augustus Begole.[32] The younger boys, W. A. and his brother Benjamin, were not living in

Mount Morris and somehow eluded the 1850 US Federal Census records entirely. Their absence suggests that they were either travelling or living where the United States Census could not find them.

Leaving home for the wild lands was a family pattern. Only three of the sixteen children who grew up together in Mount Morris stayed there. W. A.'s oldest cousin, Josiah, moved to the Michigan frontier in 1836 when he was barely twenty, followed by his brother Frederick and numerous siblings and cousins. Brother Benjamin Bradley Begole, who later called himself B.B., was by 1855 married and living in Chicago, Illinois, where he died at the age of forty-five in 1876. Considering the death of his mother and appearance in less than a year of a young stepmother, it's possible that the future San Diego City Father, William Augustus Begole, left his father's home even before 1846. To twenty-year-old W. A., mid-nineteenth-century America must have been aglitter with the promise of adventure and myriad options. He might have bunked with family in the Genesee and Livingston counties of Upstate New York where many of the Marylanders had settled, or in the more distant frontiers of Flint and Ann Arbor, Michigan, or St. Clair, Illinois, or may have chosen to seek his fortune in the American West.

# Chapter Three

## 1846–49: Nevada County, California

THERE ARE NO government records that establish W. A. Begole's whereabouts between the 1840 Federal Census and the California State Census of 1852. Records and newspapers were scarce at this time in the American West. As discussed in the previous chapter, the year of W. A. Begole's arrival in California was either 1846 or 1849. Confusion is a result of the assertion in his 1901 obituary that he had travelled west with the Donner party "in 1849" when the Donner tragedy took place in 1846. Regardless of when he arrived in California, from numerous references we can infer that he was quite likely prospecting for gold around Sacramento by 1849.

The first recorded trace of W. A. Begole in California is found in the spring of 1851 in the April 1 edition of the *Sacramento Transcript*[33] where his name appears in the *List of Letters Waiting* at the Sacramento City Post Office. Also in 1851, the Nevada County Chattel Mortgage records for May 3 show that William Augustus Begole loaned $132.16 to two miners secured by their one-tenth share in the Green Mountain Company in the long-gone Sierra "town" of Hunt's Hill.[34]

The first Begole listed in official California census records appears in the State Census of 1852. Here we find a twenty-five-year-old male Begole from New York living in Calaveras County. His occupation is "miner." Based on his unique surname, age, and birthplace this could be William Augustus. Miners were "transient and moved often to follow each new rumor of a rich strike."[35] Gold rush towns were sprouting all over central California by this time. Exactly where and when

W. A. wandered north from Calaveras to settle himself in Nevada County (established in 1851), we don't know. By the fall of 1854, though, W. A. Begole's name, along with his mining claims and partners, and general descriptions of increasing mining activity, began appearing in news and advertising in Nevada County and regional newspapers.[36] The editor of the *Nevada Journal* in October of 1854 writes,

> Having just returned from a short trip to the southern mines, I deemed it incumbent upon me to post you up what is going on here .... All we lack now is men to open and prospect the various hills about here, and show to the world that 'Red Dog is not dead yet'.... The prospects obtained the past few weeks fully sustain my statements. In Robertson's claims they get as high as six dollars to the pan in the tunnel. In Pearlman's and Begole's from three to five dollars is a very common prospect; also the same in the adjoining claims of Wooster & Morgan's, and R.&J. Chew's on Independence Hill.[37]

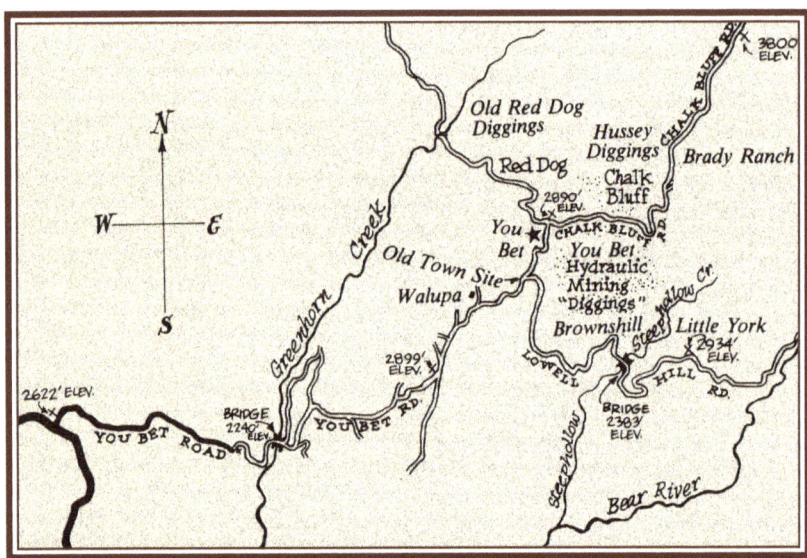

This map shows the proximity of the Nevada County gold mining towns and their "diggings." Red Dog and You Bet were barely a mile apart. Chalk Bluff and Little York, also settlements in the Little York Township, are a bit farther.[38]

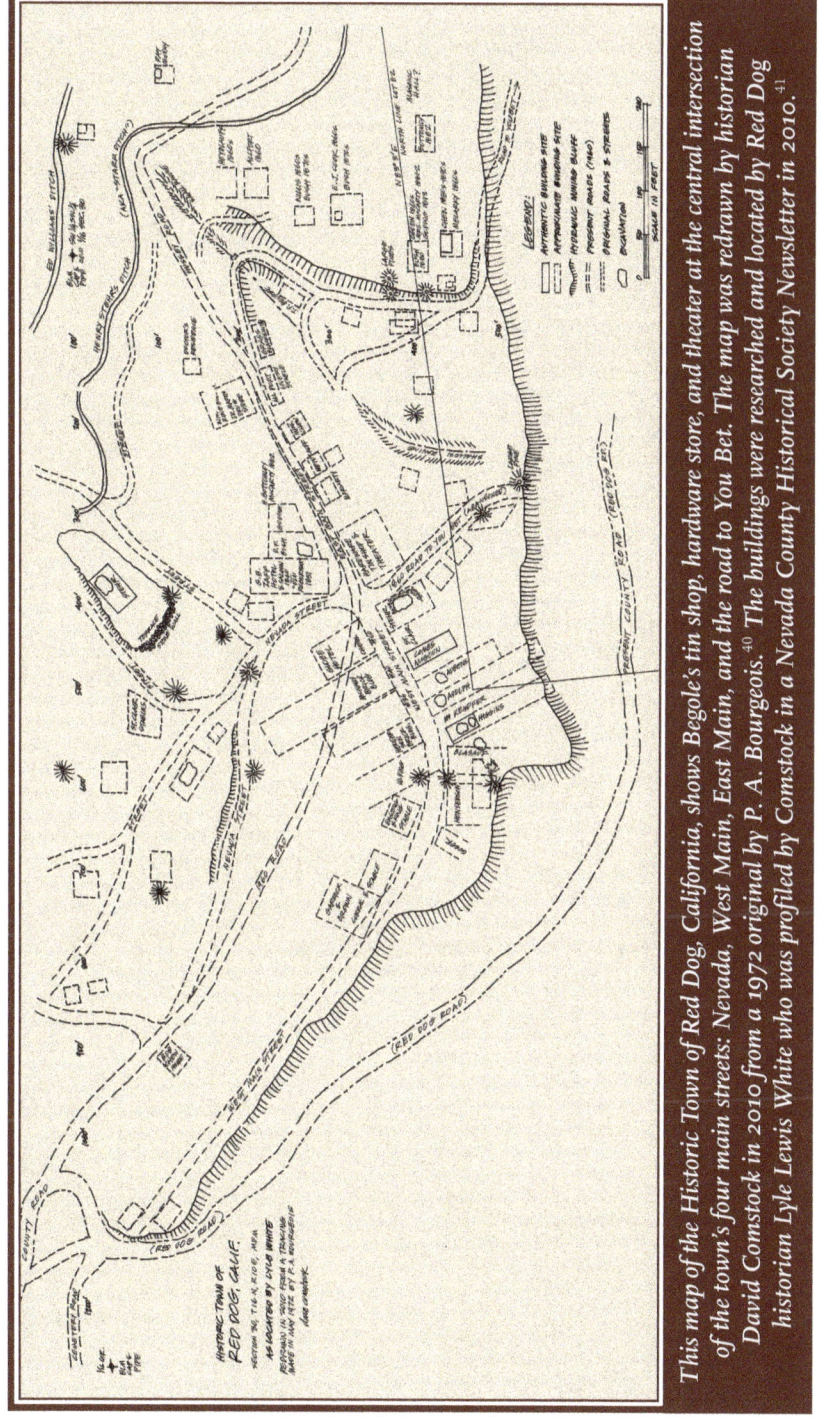

This map of the Historic Town of Red Dog, California, shows Begole's tin shop, hardware store, and theater at the central intersection of the town's four main streets: Nevada, West Main, East Main, and the road to You Bet. The map was redrawn by historian David Comstock in 2010 from a 1972 original by P. A. Bourgeois.[40] The buildings were researched and located by Red Dog historian Lyle Lewis White who was profiled by Comstock in a Nevada County Historical Society Newsletter in 2010.[41]

◇ SAN DIEGO CITY FATHER WILLIAM AUGUSTUS BEGOLE · 15

By 1855, W. A. Begole was rooted in Red Dog Diggings, Nevada County. He had learned the tinsmith trade and had established a hardware and tin shop in the center of town. (Red Dog was founded in 1850 around a gold strike near what is now Nevada City. It grew to a population of 2,000 residents before it was destroyed by fire and floods and abandoned in 1869.[39])

Beginning in November of 1855, an advertisement for the sale of W. A.'s tin shop appeared for many weeks in the Sacramento Daily Union:

> TIN SHOP FOR SALE. The subscriber having mining business to occupy his attention now offers for sale cheap for cash his Shop, Tools and Stock, situated in the town of Red Dog, Nevada County. This location is in the immediate vicinity of Waloupa, Little York, Dutch Flat, Lowell Hill, Remington Hill, Steep Hollow and Greenhorn Creeks, all good mining places. Any persons desirous of going into the business in the mountains would do well to call on the subscriber before locating elsewhere. WM. A BEGOLE.[42]

While these ads evidently failed to attract a buyer for the tin shop, (W. A. Begole completed his 300-seat theater in Red Dog on this property in 1861 and still owned the property twelve years later when it was destroyed by fire), they identify W. A. Begole as a Red Dog property and business owner. Combined with articles and mentions in local newspapers around the same time, these provide the earliest traces of W. A.'s business, mining, and political activities in and around Little York and Red Dog. He is just shy of thirty years old and unattached when he begins to leave a trail in the new State of California. Mention of mining interests in the spring of 1855 precede November 1855 advertising of the tin shop, suggesting that W. A. Begole was likely living and working in Red Dog before 1855.

* The *Nevada Journal* reports in January 1855, as hydraulic mining is getting underway in Nevada County, that, "Messrs. Pearlman and Begole on Independence Hill, took out $205 with the labor of two men, and this is only prospecting."[43]

* In May 1855, the *Nevada Journal* lists "Begole and Crane" as one of seven companies engaged in hydraulic mining in Red Dog and being supplied with water from the Chalk Bluff Ditch.[44] Just a month later, in a public notice in the same newspaper, Wm. A. Begole is listed with his mining partner Dr. D. A. Crane, a physician, and two others, John Lobdell and T. R. Morgan, as owners of the Steep Hollow Canal Company which intends to supply water to hydraulic mining operations in "Walloupa, Red Dog, Mule Ravine and intermediate places."[45]
* By the spring of 1856, the *Nevada Journal* reports that an "order of Red Men" has been instituted at Red Dog and that W. A. Begole and his mining partner Dr. D. A. Crane are among the five officers.[46] Comstock writes, "As genuine Nisenan became fewer in the country, ersatz Indians were created to take their places. Along with their lands, the Americans began taking their names. In February 1856, when the Order of Red Men established its first California lodge at the mining camp at Red Dog, the charter members named their chapter "Wehmeh" No. 1. The neighboring camp of Walloupa already had taken the name of Wema's subchief, Waloupa."[47]
* That summer (1856), W. A. Begole, again with his mining partner Dr. D. A. Crane, is one of eight Red Dog "boys" elected delegates to the County Convention of the American Party, also known as the "Know Nothing" party (for its members' and sympathizers' disclaimers of affiliation with the party's nativist creed and its anti-immigrant and anti-Catholic activities). The American Party split at its National Convention later that summer, its anti-slavery faction emerging as the new Republican Party.
* In January of 1857, W. A. Begole's cohort in several business ventures, political activities and fraternal clubs, Dr. D. A. Crane, was shot, not fatally, in the chest by William Langston during an argument in W. A.'s Red Dog tin shop. Langston escaped.[48]
* The 1856–7 edition of *Hutchings Illustrated*[49] reports W. A.'s invention of a "sheet iron penstock" that contains water at much higher pressure, blasting cement hills around Little York to

even greater smithereens. Though hydraulic cement mining was eventually outlawed for its environmental devastation, in the late 1850s more powerful blasting was considered a significant technological "improvement."

* In 1857, the *Sacramento Union* reports that Begole & Company claims are "paying big"[50] and that W. A. Begole was elected a Justice of the Peace for the township of Little York.[51] A newspaper article reports "Justice Begole" adjudicating a Red Dog shooting in 1858.[52]

* In the spring of 1858 Begole and Johnson erected a cement crushing mill on the old Rogers and Company claims in Little York "which was a considerable improvement on its predecessor."[53]

* That summer, in August of 1858, during the run-up to the contentious presidential election of 1860 and ultimately the American Civil War, W. A. Begole was elected a delegate to the Independent Convention in Nevada, representing the township of Little York. Eschewing both Whig and Democratic parties for their stance on slavery, W. A.'s participation in nominating "independent" candidates at this divisive time in the nation's history is the beginning of what becomes his lifetime affiliation with Abraham Lincoln's Republican Party.[54]

* According to Bean's History and Directory of Nevada County,[55] 1858 was also the year that W. A. Begole and his partner E. B. Johnson bought up and consolidated claims known as the "Blue Lead" in Little York and erected a ten-stamp mill on them. By December of that same year, the Blue Lead was running eight stamps continuously, producing "fine specimens" of cement and gold, paying about $8 a ton.[56]

* Nevada County Deeds and Chattel Mortgages show that W. A. was actively buying and selling mining claims, mining facilities, and other properties, making loans and taking mining claims as collateral, and forming business partnerships in Red Dog, Chalk Bluff, and other towns in and around Little York Township between 1859 and 1866.[57] (In May of 1860 W. A. loaned merchant John J. Adolph the money to buy a portion of W. A.'s property on Red Dog's Main Street.[58])

* In the middle of this activity, during the summer of 1860, for reasons we don't know, perhaps just a visit back "home," W. A. Begole sailed for New York. His name was on the passenger lists of the *S.S. Sonora* leaving San Francisco for Panama in early July, and on the *S.S. Northern Light* leaving from Aspinwall, Panama, to arrive in New York on August 2. Prior to the completion of the Pacific Railroad nine years later, this was the fastest of the three methods of coast-to-coast travel available, with the overland and Cape Horn routes often taking many months to complete. (The "Panama Route" usually took three to four weeks.)
* The next year, in April 1861, W. A. completed the building of a 300-seat theater on his Main Street property,[59] and in August he was listed as a board member of the newly formed Red Dog Fire Department.

## 1860s: Red Dog Ventures Sweet and Sour

The 1860s in Red Dog were cluttered with natural and man-made disasters and business disappointments. Fire was a familiar destroyer of mining towns and mining operations. The first of several fires to devastate Red Dog occurred on January 15, 1859, burning Main Street buildings, killing one man who burned to death in his saloon, and destroying about $25,000 worth of property.[60]

Records are murky in determining whether Begole and Johnson's "Blue Lead Mine" venture was a success, a flop, or something in between. A real estate listing for the Blue Lead Gold Mine in March 2012 (asking price $4.2 million) asserts that, "the site was extensively hydraulically mined during the late 1800s to the early 1900s during which they recovered millions of dollars of gold. While Nevada County has produced more gold than any other county in California, the Red Dog/You Bet mining district was the richest producing district in the County."[61] However, Bean's *History of 1867*[62] reports that yield at the Blue Lead varied significantly across just a few years, that the 1858 stamping mills were "insufficient for the work intended," but that later washings and re-washings of the tailings "yielded tens of thousands." Bean also reports about the Blue Lead that during "the time they ran the mill they took out between sixty and seventy-thousand dollars, never made a dividend, and quit in debt."

Newspaper records report that 1861 was a difficult year for W. A. Begole. In March 1861, W. A.'s business partner, saloon keeper, and miner William Quirk, another native of New York, was found dead, buried under a cave-in at his Red Dog claim.[63] Quirk was buried in the Red Dog Cemetery. (In 1862, W. A. purchased from Quirk's estate Quirk's half of the Red Dog Water Works as well as his share of the Couts-Quirk mining claim.[64])

The following October, the Blue Lead Mine venture ended abruptly and likely unprofitably for W. A. Begole and E. B. Johnson. Both Bean and the *Sacramento Union* on October 17 report W. A.'s crushing mill at Little York—presumably the Blue Lead Mine operation—as destroyed by a fire that began in the blacksmith shop.[65]

The Little York fire was followed by record-setting rainfalls that flooded central California, beginning in December 1861. In a Christmas Day letter to California Surveyor General J. F. Houghton, W. A. Begole encloses his own precise measurements of daily rainfall between the end of December 1861 and June 1862, a total of 79.53 inches, and the information that it rained about 30 inches before he started measuring. On the anniversary of the deluge, a year later, the *Sacramento Daily Union* reported, "On this coast, no similar floods, judging from the absence of all evidence of their presence, have been experienced for a century, and in all probability, a century may again pass before another such a winter as the last will be experienced in California."[66]

Despite these formidable setbacks, a few intrepid Red Dog men with Masonic ties shared enough faith in their town's future to establish a Masonic Lodge. Mount Carmel Lodge No. 155 was instituted on May 27, 1862, and received its charter a year later, on May 14, 1863. William A. Begole was a charter member, serving as senior warden to start. During the ten years of the Mount Carmel Lodge's existence, W. A. would serve two terms as master,[67] a pattern of fraternal devotion that continued in San Diego.

Newspaper records are quiet until 1864. In June and September that year, the *Daily Alta California* reported an auction of W. A.'s shares in the Guadalupe de Los Angeles Gold and Silver Mining Company of Durango, Mexico,[68] suggesting that his mining interests at one time extended beyond Alta, California and that he ran out of money or lost interest in some of them.

In November 1864, W. A. Begole was commissioned by Governor Frederick Low, a Senior Second Lieutenant in the Little York Union Guard, Fourth Brigade, California Militia/National Guard. The Little York Union Guard was established in Dall's Saloon in the neighboring town of You Bet by the petition of local residents for a voluntary company. According to the Little York Union Guard history, "This small settlement was full of patriotic fervor during the War of Rebellion."[69] However, California's connection with that great conflict was minor.[70] The Little York Union Guard history further reports much ado about acquiring military uniforms and functioning swords, the loss of a drummer and fifer, and enjoying splendid military training for ten days at Camp Kibbe, but it makes no mention of military engagement of any sort during the war or after. The Union Guard's history states: "The mining districts of the State at this time were inhabited by a more or less transient population, and even though the company was well equipped both in arms and uniforms after the close of the War of Rebellion, patriotic fervor subsided to such an extent that the National Guard units suffered a relapse in membership."[71] The company was mustered out after the war ended.

As late as February 1866, still presumably optimistic about mining in the area, W. A. was still purchasing additional mining claims.[72]

## *1866: Red Dog Destroyed by Fire, W. A. Begole Rebuilds*

The dates of the next two calamitous fires in the town of Red Dog are recorded differently by secondary and primary sources. Both Wells' History of Nevada County and the 1867 edition of *Bean's History and Directory*, secondary sources, cite 1862 for both fires. "In June, 1862 a fire burned the Chinese portion of the town, and on the 15th of the following August the entire town was completely destroyed in less than half an hour, some sixty houses being burned."[73,74] However, the August catastrophe was more likely in 1866 as reported in the *San Francisco Bulletin* on August 18, 1866 (citing the *Nevada County Transcript* of August 17). *The Bulletin* reported losses at $50,000 from the fire that started at three in the afternoon in the Pavilion Hotel on Main Street and spread rapidly to every part of town, burning both sides of Main Street and crossing the ravine east of town to burn several dwellings. Only one brick building in the principal part of town survived the fire: "The flames spread so rapidly that in many instances the occupants of the buildings were unable even to save their clothing, and a large amount of coin was lost from the drawers and elsewhere." Among the buildings and businesses lost was W. A. Begole's "theater and hardware store" valued at $5,000, for which he was compensated $1,000 by the insurer, Pacific Company. A few other properties were also insured by the Pacific and Occidental insurance companies, but most were not.[75]

A year later, according to Bean's 1867 *History and Directory of Nevada County*, the 200 intrepid inhabitants of Red Dog had soldiered past another ruinous event,

> ... with that characteristic energy that marks Californians, whom no calamity can subdue. They immediately rebuilt the town and it now presents a better appearance than ever before. The business of the place is not as extensive now as heretofore, nevertheless it has a more healthy and solid foundation on account of the settled permanency of the population.

All of Red Dog, except Heydlauff's store, built of brick, was raised in a year from the ashes, impressive progress for a tiny town of only 200 people.

> There are here at present two general variety stores, kept respectively by J. Heydlauff and McGoun & Combs. Both of these stores also buy gold dust, the former for himself, and the latter

for the enterprising bankers, Mackie & Philip, of Nevada. There are also two clothing stores; one hardware and tin shop [this likely belonging to W. A. Begole]; one shoemaker shop; one butcher shop; two hotels; three saloons; two fruit and liquor stands; one dressmaker, and one blacksmith shop. There are also two halls in the town—one belonging to the Masons, in which they meet every Friday on or preceding the full moon; the other belonging to the Odd Fellows, in which they meet every Saturday night. There is daily communication by stage with Nevada and Colfax. There is also a residence of the Justice of the Peace and Constable for Little York Township. There are four mills within a short distance of Red Dog for crushing blue cement .... The hydraulic claims are all being worked, and promise a good yield of gold this season.[76]

The Masonic meeting hall in this description must belong to Mount Carmel Lodge, the only one in town. Mount Carmel's membership peaked in 1867 at 36. Evidently members raised funds to build a 24-by-48-foot meeting hall on the east side of Main Street that was mentioned in the *Dutch Flat Weekly Enquirer* in the spring of that year.[77]

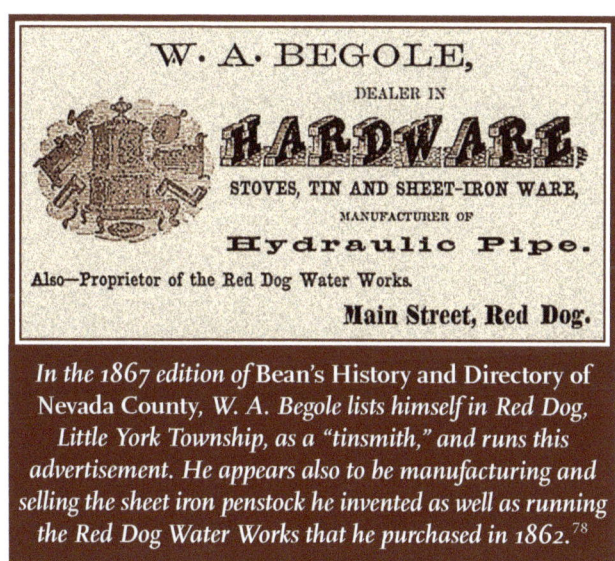

*In the 1867 edition of* Bean's History and Directory of Nevada County, *W. A. Begole lists himself in Red Dog, Little York Township, as a "tinsmith," and runs this advertisement. He appears also to be manufacturing and selling the sheet iron penstock he invented as well as running the Red Dog Water Works that he purchased in 1862.*[78]

## 1867–68: Red Dog Succumbs to Deluge and Exhausted Mining

The final "swallowing" of Red Dog by its neighboring mining settlement of You Bet, a mile away, was a result of several factors:

* More than one hundred days of continuous heavy rains during the winter of 1867–68 washed away hydraulic ditches and flumes, destroyed the water supply that was essential for the town's mining operations, and buried mining equipment and rich "pay dirt" under tons of mud and debris.[79,80]
* Hydraulic mining in Red Dog was no longer profitable for small operators. Engineering expertise and equipment required to create outlets for the vast hills and rivers of tailings that had been produced by hydraulic mining and to purchase and operate the "improved appliances" required to extract more gold from the tailings were beyond the reach of all but the largest companies of "capitalist" investors. Hydraulic mining in the Red Dog area would continue until the Sawyer Decision in 1884 ended the practice because of its profound environmental destruction and danger to downstream settlements and farms.[81]
* The town of You Bet was nearly completely destroyed by fire on April 24, 1869[82] and in need of buildings.

On November 13, 1869, a "Brief Item" in the *Sacramento Daily Union* announced, "Red Dog is no more; You Bet has swallowed it."[83] The post office at Red Dog closed four days later, exactly fourteen years after it had opened on February 17, 1855. The last few remaining members of the Mount Carmel Masonic Lodge surrendered their charter on August 16, 1872. Lodge records were lost in the 1906 Great Fire in San Francisco. Some sources report as many as 2,000 people—men, women, and children—during Red Dog's heyday. But those numbers had already dwindled to only a few hundred souls after the fires and rains of the late 1860s.

Wells recalls in his *History of Nevada County*, published in 1880, that "nearly all the houses, including the Odd Fellows Hall, were moved to You Bet, which then became the live town of the district. There are now but the unoccupied brick store and one other building standing on the old site of the town of Red Dog."[84] Juanita Brown writes that the Odd Fellows Hall was the last building to be moved, and that occurred in 1870.[85] Today (2016), nothing of Red Dog remains but the old Red Dog Cemetery, maintained by the Nevada County Cemetery District.

The Boston Hydraulic Gold Mine in Red Dog, circa 1879. This mine was located east of Red Dog, about a quarter of a mile from Greenhorn Creek. The photograph was taken by renowned San Francisco photographer Carleton E. Watkins who was touring the Northern Mines as a commercial photographer. He aimed to promote modern industrial mining methods and man's technological conquest of nature in the pursuit of gold.[86]

Histories, newspaper articles, and public records show that the town of Red Dog was destroyed during the winter of 1868 and abandoned completely by 1870. Even so, there is a trace of evidence that W. A. Begole kept one foot in Nevada County at the same time he moved south to San Diego. W. A. was elected high priest of the Nevada Royal Arch Masons No. 6 in Nevada City, California, in December of 1868, and he registered to vote as a resident of Red Dog on August 3, 1869, the same day his deed for the double lot at 529 Fifth Street was recorded in San Diego County. Six weeks later, he steamed into San Diego.

# Chapter Four

## 1869: New Beginning in San Diego

SAN DIEGO, IN the fall of 1869, was transforming quickly from a sleepy seaside outpost into a speculative frenzy as a result of the well-hyped expectation that the transcontinental railroad would steam into town any minute and make everybody rich. William Augustus Begole, forty-three years old, arrived in San Diego on September 24 with gold coin in his pocket, Masonic connections, a trade and business that benefited from growth and building, and bona fide Republican credentials. W. A.'s arrival was within a few weeks of W. W. Bowers, Alonzo Horton's brother-in-law; Horton's parents, and close behind A. E. Horton himself and a few other New Town notables: *San Diego Union* publisher-editors Ed Bushyhead and father and son Lewis C. and Douglas Gunn; freight forwarder Aaron Pauley; cattleman Warren Hackett; the lawyer brothers Daniel and William Cleveland, and merchant and Fifth Street neighbor Joseph Nash. W. A. was a few years ahead of lawyer Chalmers Scott, who became the county recorder, and merchants Simon Levi, George Marston, and William Wallace Stewart.

These men and others—all "Sixty-Niners" and founders and promoters of "New Town" San Diego, whose names are familiar even to casual students of San Diego history—would become W. A. Begole's lifelong friends, Masonic brothers, Republican Party allies, fellow civic leaders, business associates, and customers.

During his thirty years in San Diego, W. A. Begole served the growing city in a number and variety of different capacities and roles though the boom times and the busts. Although he listed his occupation as a "capitalist" for a few years after he retired and may have profited from a few real estate investments and mining ventures, the evidence suggests he supported himself modestly with his work as a tinsmith and hardware dealer. For all his years in San Diego, he lived over the store at 529 Fifth Street, even as Lower Fifth declined from its 1870s pinnacle when it was the heart of Horton's bright New Town. Three decades later, the bright New Town had forsaken its waterfront. By the late 1890s, W. A. Begole's handsome brick shop with the "fine iron front, large show windows and galvanized iron cornice"[87] overlooked the jumble of saloons, gambling halls, and red-light amusements of San Diego's notorious "Stingaree."

W. A. Begole's activities, pursuits, and alliances in San Diego satisfied his mercantile and civic aspirations, and reflected the city's booms and busts. He had no obvious prior connections to Horton, Bowers, Marston, Bushyhead, the Gunns, or any of the enterprising newcomers who hoped to prosper with San Diego's development. Even so, W. A. slid seemingly easily into the political and civic power structure that was emerging with Horton's vision. His past alliances and enterprises no doubt helped smooth the way. (San Diego's Old Town leaders were mainly Democrats, even Southern-sympathizing "Copperheads." Devout Republican Alonzo Horton, however, made known that he would employ only his own kind and would turn San Diego from a "Democratic hole" into a Republican one.[88])

## 1870s: Sliding Into the "New Boys" Network — Start-Up Real Estate, Mining, Politics, Civic, and Fraternal Endeavors
### "Everybody was in the real estate business."

Elizabeth MacPhail writes that in the early 1870s, stirred by the promise of a railroad link between San Diego's near-perfect harbor and the rest of the continent, everybody in San Diego was investing in real estate[89] and other ventures to support development and trade. W. A. Begole arrived in town having already purchased the double lot on Fifth Street.

By winter, he had also become a stockholder in the Fort Yuma Road Company, filed the first of his half-dozen Julian and Pine Valley mining claims, and had been recommended for affiliation with Masonic Lodge No. 35 by William Cleveland and S. W. Craigue.[90]

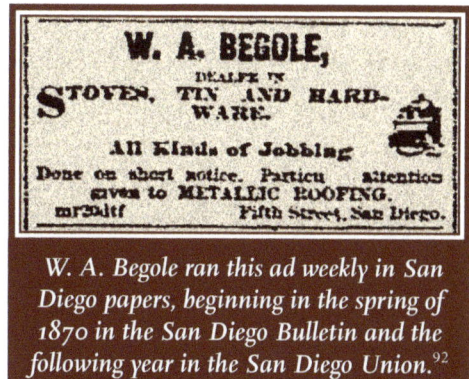

W. A. Begole ran this ad weekly in San Diego papers, beginning in the spring of 1870 in the San Diego Bulletin and the following year in the San Diego Union.[92]

By Spring 1870, W. A. Begole was regularly advertising his Fifth Street business, "Stoves, Tin and Hardware and All Kinds of Jobbing," in the *San Diego Bulletin*. He had also purchased directly from A. E. Horton a second lot on Sixth Street in Horton's Addition, and a third from real estate agent Colonel G. G. Bradt.[91]

## *The Brotherhood of Freemasonry*

After being elected to affiliate in the spring of 1870, in December of that year, W. A. Begole was elected Master of San Diego Masonic Lodge No. 35, F and A. M., a position he held for the next five years and assumed again in 1885. The immediate previous master was William H. Cleveland, the Old Town lawyer who had sponsored W. A.'s affiliation.

Masonic Lodge No. 35 was the first lodge in Southern California. It was established in the 1850s by a few early-bird San Diego promoters who invested in the always-imminent railroad and realized there were enough Masons in good standing in San Diego to apply for a dispensation. One of these men was William Heath Davis, the original New Town visionary/land speculator and San Francisco millionaire who invested $60,000 to build the first wharf. A second founder of Lodge No. 35 was John Judson Ames, a Mainer originally, gold miner, jack of many San Francisco enterprises, and proprietor/publisher of San Diego's first newspaper, the *Herald*. From his San Diego History Center biography, J. Judson Ames "cast his lot with the new town (Graytown or Davis's Folly) which was then just starting." Ames had met Davis in San Francisco, where "he had formed a number of valuable friendships, especially among his Masonic brethren."[93]

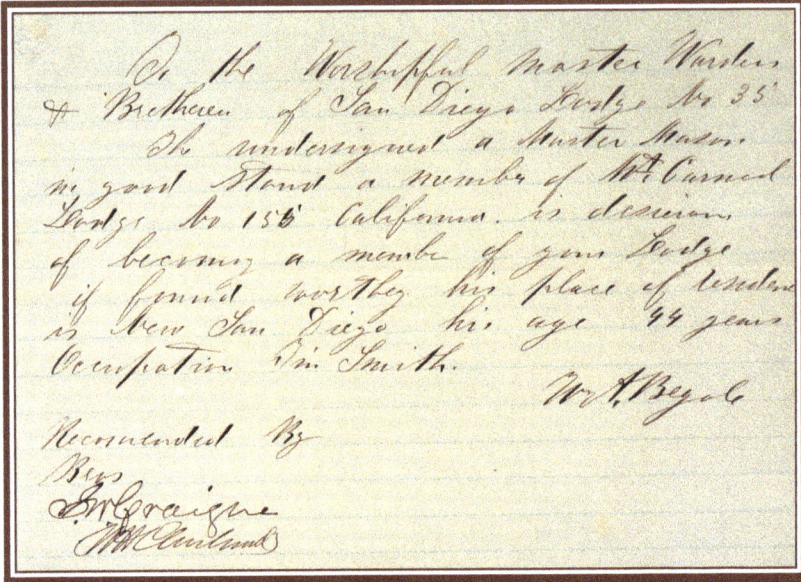

W. A. Begole applied for election to membership in Masonic Lodge No. 35 in February 1870, just a few months after he arrived in San Diego. His sponsors were merchant Solomon W. Craigue and lawyer William H. Cleveland, whose signatures also appear on this application card. W. A. was elected a member "by affiliation" in March 1870 "demitting from the Mount Carmel Lodge No. 155" which W. A. had co-founded in Red Dog.

Orion Zink, Lodge Historian of San Diego Lodge No. 35 wrote in the 1970s:

> It has often been said that the history of San Diego Lodge is almost a history of San Diego itself. Due of course to the fact that so many of its members played such important parts in the City's civic, industrial, cultural and spiritual growth. These were men of stature, all of whom left their mark, and aided in transforming San Diego from a sleepy Mexican pueblo to the thriving city we are privileged to live in today.[94]

Among the Masters and members of San Diego Lodge No. 35 between 1860 and 1900 are men whose familiar names dominate San Diego's primary historical records and secondary histories. We find Louis Rose, William Ferrell, Agostin Haraszthy, James W. Robinson, George Derby, Philip Crosthwaite, E. W. Morse, James Robinson, Daniel Kurtz, Thomas Darnell, George Pendleton, Marcus Schiller, Joseph Manasse, Frederick N. Pauley, Chalmers Scott, Simon Levi, Abraham Klauber, William Cleveland, Solon William Craigue, Alonzo Horton, G. G. Bradt, Ed Bushyhead, Douglas Gunn, Samuel Warren Hackett, W. W. Bowers, W. J. Hunsaker, and Daniel Cave, to name just a few.

Whether local Masonic leaders of the 1860s and '70s knew one another in San Francisco or somewhere else before they arrived in San Diego is possible but undocumented. Once in San Diego, however, the Masonic brothers interacted from leadership positions in their fraternal organization and across the spectrum of business and civic enterprises, social affairs, political endeavors, assignments, activities, appointments, and elected offices. They were the city builders. This pattern is recognized with pride in Masonic histories, such as this one about the Grand Lodge of California:

> The history of the Grand Lodge of California is inseparable from the history of the State of California. Those same brave pioneers who came west in search of wealth, fame, and opportunity came to bring their beloved fraternity, and all that it entails, with them. In some cases, bringing Masonry to 'The New Frontier' was their primary purpose. Grand Masters of Eastern jurisdictions issued Charters to western-bound sojourners, giving them the right to work as Lodges in the Wild West, under the jurisdiction of the Eastern Grand Lodge. Other Grand Masters issued Dispensations, giving groups of Masons who found themselves in this Masonic Wilderness the right to meet and organize as California Masonic Lodges.
>
> In 1849, gold was discovered near Sutter's Mill. Word quickly moved eastward and men accordingly began to move west. Such a long, difficult and dangerous journey is not to be

undertaken lightly, or alone. Men seeking their fortunes knew that to go it alone was an invitation to disaster. Accordingly, they banded together into traveling parties, and sought ways to fulfill the need for fraternalism and mutual assistance. Some had long been Masons, others joined Masonic Lodges, and together, as Brethren, they made their way West.

It is unsurprising therefore, that many prominent leaders in this new frontier were members of our fraternity. With the number of Masons, and the prominence the Craft played in their lives and the lives of others, the obvious action was to create a Grand Lodge of Masons in California.[95]

*These Masonic Officers' Jewels were created by W. A. Begole in his tin shop and were used by Lodge No. 35 officers during his terms in office, 1871–1875, and 1885. Lodge No. 35 legend says that these were the first jewels used by their officers. The forms are based on architectural instruments and symbolize Masonic principles of proper and balanced action and behavior. Begole's hand-crafted tin jewels are still on display in the office of Lodge No. 35 in San Diego.*

W. A. Begole's dedication for thirty years to San Diego Masonry shows that this affiliation was primary and meant more to him than a springboard to local prominence. In addition to his long association with Masonic Lodge No. 35, W. A. also founded two other San Diego Masonic groups: Royal Arch Masons Chapter No. 61, where he served as high priest in the years 1883, 1884, 1886, 1888, and 1889; and San Diego

York Rite Commandery No. 25 Knights Templar. For W. A. Begole, the growth and development of these organizations and their individual members seems to have been an end in itself. He served in countless leadership and support positions for these endeavors and remained a contributing member until his death. Virtually every Mason in San Diego during this period could recall the evening that W. A. Begole had helped initiate him into the order.

The impressive funeral performed by W. A.'s Masonic brothers in 1901 was predicted accurately by the *San Union Tribune* to be "the largest turnout of Masons that the city has ever known." The presence of more than 200 brothers reflected their respect, admiration and affection for their oldest member. The *San Diego Union* wrote in their account of his funeral and burial in the Masonic plot at Mount Hope cemetery that the organization had been his wife and family for all the years he had devoted his energy to its up-building.[96] (But for a brief marriage in 1881 that ended in divorce a year later, and an older brother in Kansas, W. A. Begole had no other immediate family.) His Masonic brothers were his pallbearers. Lodge No. 35 Master Samuel Smith was the executor of his estate and the lodge a beneficiary of his will.

Nevertheless, in keeping with so many Masonic histories, W. A. also benefitted professionally from his Masonic relational network. Innumerable of W.A's projects, business interests, civic associations, and public positions for the next thirty years were linked in some way to one or another of his Masonic brethren.

## *Public Service and Private Enterprise*

Based upon W. A. Begole's persistent presence in San Diego business, political, and civic circles for three decades, his absence from published histories is something of a mystery. Except for his name on official lists, such as the list of city trustees or aldermen; lists of Mason masters; and lists of board members of various institutions and clubs, he rarely receives even a mention in the familiar histories of San Diego: Van Dyke, Smythe, MacPhail, Pourade, Engstrand, or Crawford.[97] Even

Richard Pourade's extensive seven-volume *History of San Diego* refers to him just once (in volume four, *The Glory Years,* chapter "Gunfight at Campo"). Pourade writes that Begole was a member of the committee who rode to Campo to dampen a smoldering incident at the Mexican border. Other members of the posse, like Begole all city fathers of an official sort, were Ephraim Morse, William W. Bowers, William Wallace Stewart, Allan Klauber, Harry Hill Wildy, Douglas Gunn, and Charles A. Wetmore.

*The Campo gunfight began at Lumen and Silas Gaskill's store in Campo, shown here in the 1880s.*

W. A. Begole is one of three members of that posse that the Pourade series does not discuss in any other context; the other two are H. H. Wildy and W. W. Stewart. At that time, he was finishing his fifth year as Master of Masonic Lodge No. 35 and was one of the five San Diego city trustees, elected from the Third Ward in 1873, about to take his turn as president of that board, a position roughly equivalent to that of mayor. Morse was a former San Diego city trustee, a prominent city merchant and active leader of the new San Diego Chamber of Commerce, and that year, the San Diego public administrator. Bowers was Alonzo Horton's brother-in-law, had supervised the construction of Horton House, begun a career in public office with his election to the California Assembly, and was that year serving as the collector of customs at the port of San Diego. Wildy was the San Diego District Attorney. Gunn was the proprietor/manager of the *San Diego Union*. Stewart and Klauber were merchants prominent in civic and political affairs. Charles Wetmore was a "Special US Commissioner of Mission Indians."

During the boom-then-bust years leading to the1875 Campo Gunfight, W. A. grew his San Diego roots. Evidently they were deep enough to keep him in the city despite the 1873 bank failure, which, for the next decade, quashed the promise of the Texas Pacific railroad connection. Railroad financing and everything tied to it fell apart. As steamers full of newcomers quit coming, land sales disappeared, speculators and hangers-on crashed and left town, and the population dropped from 5,000 to 1,500.[98]

A dedicated core troupe stuck by San Diego and set about city building. Among this cluster of community boosters, who in down times initiated so many of San Diego's foundational institutions and enterprises, was W. A. Begole. However, as his absence in San Diego's history texts suggests, W. A. was backstage much more often than he was in the spotlight. He was mostly a work-a-day, support-role kind of guy, rarely the luminary at the dais. For example, he was a trustee of the San Diego Reading Room, a delegate to the Republican County Convention, vice president of the Citizens Railroad Committee, nominated for president of the Grant-Wilson Club (San Diegans supporting the election of Ulysses Grant to the US presidency), a grand juror, a trustee of the San Diego Library, and chairman of the Republican County Committee, and a member of the Honorary Committee for the 1874 Fireman's Ball.

W. A.'s name was also frequently on passenger lists of steamers that travelled between San Diego, Los Angeles, and San Francisco, sometimes accompanied by his friend Douglas Gunn. A scattering of news bits in Los Angeles and San Francisco newspapers during this time cite hotel arrivals, property transactions in both cities, and stagecoach trips between the two, but it has been difficult to flesh out these suggestions of ongoing business dealings beyond San Diego.

# CHAPTER FIVE

*Between Booms: Mid 1870s to the Early 1880s*

IN HER BOOK, *The Story of San Diego and Its Founder Alonzo Horton*, Elizabeth MacPhail writes a detailed history of San Diego in the last quarter of the nineteenth century, entitling the period between 1874 and 1879, "Living on Climate and Great Expectations":

> The next decade (after the 1873 financial panic) in San Diego was a period of marking time. Those who were retired or had come for their health were content to live on climate and savings.... Others who remained stayed because they liked it here and, like Horton, were confident that because of its climate and bay San Diego would one day be a great city. They were willing to wait, time and again being buoyed up by promises of great things to come, meaning a railroad .... There were no society 'greats.' Each individual was accepted for himself, without regard to his background or financial condition.[99]

Between booms—despite empty buildings, lack of commerce, drought, and increasing ethnic animosities toward the Chinese and Native Americans—the population grew slowly. In the county, agriculture grew, particularly fruit and honey production, and gold mining tanked. Pourade calls these years the "Discontented Seventies" and writes, "Life was rather serene, though it was not always easy to live with thoughts of what might have been, and picnics were a favorite pastime. They were held under the great oaks or pepper trees, which were growing everywhere, in town and country, and buckboard buffets dispensed the bounties of the good seasons."[100]

W. A. Begole built a small and sturdy tin trunk in 1876 for safekeeping of Lodge No. 35 financial records. Still stuffed with folders, one for each year from 1876 to 1900, the trunk remains in the proud custody of Lodge No. 35.

San Diegans during the Discontented Seventies continued bit by bit to create the city's mechanical, commercial, civic, cultural, and political infrastructure. The city trustees had already set aside 1,440 acres for what is now Balboa Park and had established Mount Hope Cemetery.

There was already a courthouse and a post office. A water company formed in San Diego drilled wells and pumped water to a reservoir at Fifth and Hawthorne. The city secured federal funds to channel the San Diego River back into False (now Mission) Bay when the rains came.[101] Board sidewalks and the first fire hydrant appeared on Fifth Street. In the winter of 1874, the San Diego Fire Department threw an Annual Ball at Horton's Hall, and W. A. Begole was on the Honorary and Reception Committees with twenty-five other local luminaries. The San Diego Society of Natural History was founded by Daniel Cleveland and Dr. George Barnes, and W. A. Begole served as Recording Secretary. The new Commercial Bank opened on the corner of Fifth and G Streets, and W. A. Begole built its tin roof. The San Diego Free Reading Room Association opened San Diego's first library, and W. A. Begole was a trustee and served on the Board of Managers. A gas company came to town. George Marston opened his own store on the corner of Fifth and D and married Anna Lee Gunn, Douglas Gunn's sister; George Marston and Douglas Gunn' father, Lewis Gunn, were the witnesses at W. A. Begole's 1881 marriage to Helen E. Hanford. The first City Directory was published by the Chamber of Commerce in 1874. W. A. Begole was listed and advertised in the directory, and for the next three years he was a vice president of the Chamber.

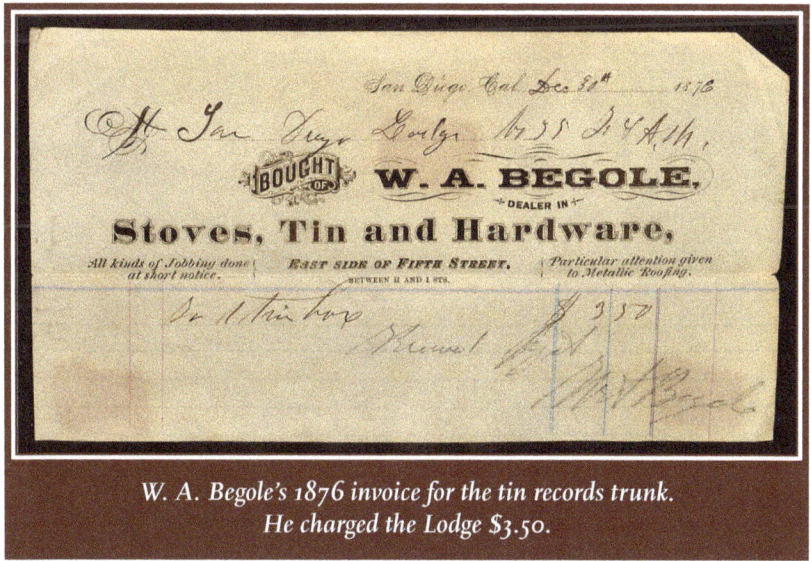

W. A. Begole's 1876 invoice for the tin records trunk. He charged the Lodge $3.50.

During this decade, W. A. Begole also served two terms (1873–1877) as one of five San Diego City Trustees.[102] While he was president of the trustees (February 1875–May 1876), he received the once-again disappointing cable from Washington, D.C., that announced postponement of a vote to subsidize the Texas Pacific railroad's link to San Diego. During his tenure, the Southern Pacific Railroad finally connected San Francisco and Los Angeles, allowing San Diegans to hang onto their vision of connecting their magnificent harbor with the rest of the continent. (For a detailed account of the thirty-year railroad saga that provoked and perpetuated San Diego's land booms and busts, see the pamphlet, "The Railroad Story of San Diego County."[103])

In August 1873, the same year W. A. began his term as a San Diego city trustee, his second cousin, Charles Dorrance (also spelled Dorrence) Begole of Lone Pine, another member of this intrepid generation that settled the American West, with two companions (A. H. Johnson and J. Lucas) became "the first to climb Mount Whitney."[104]

It was also during his City Trustees presidency that W. A. Begole designed and raised the funds to build a "party cannon" (in the photograph at the front of this book) for San Diego's enthusiastic celebration of the nation's 100$^{th}$ birthday on July 4, 1876.[105] This parade and festival accoutrement was parked on its caisson in Horton Plaza for many years and was known both as "The Little Slogan" and "the Centennial Gun." The cannon, which disappeared in the 1920s, was recovered in 2014 and restored in 2016 by San Diego's Save Our Heritage Organisation and members of the Begole family.

## 529 *Fifth Street: W. A.'s "Home Office"*

Another of W. A. Begole's achievements during the late 1870s was upgrading the building at 529 Fifth Street on the east side between Island and Market, where he lived and worked.

In 1878, the *San Diego Union* reported the completion of W. A.'s new brick building on the south portion of his double lot at 529 Fifth Street, "a handsome store with a fine iron front, large shop windows and galvanized iron cornices."[106] The San Diego Gaslamp Association features the Higgins–Begole Building on their "Gaslamp Quarter Architectural and History Tour" which GeoTourist has posted online. The tour itinerary explains the building's evolution:

> Two separate buildings were joined in a single façade before 1921. The north half building's first story was constructed circa 1868, the oldest documented brick building in the Gaslamp Quarter. W. A. Begole, who ran the hardware store, added a second story in 1878 and a third in 1886. The south two-story art deco building was constructed by Mr. Higgins in 1873 and a third story added between 1906 and 1921 when the facades were joined. It served as a grocery, dry goods and billiard parlor. The upper floors were rented rooms, most likely a bordello before the 1912 Stingaree raid. It also served as rooms for the Salvation Army, the Hotel Togo and the Hawaiian Hotel.[107]

## *The Republican Advantage*

To be a Republican was an advantage in 1870s San Diego. Horton's ambition to shape his city's political preferences was well known, and Republican committees and clubs were prolific and active. W. A. Begole had been actively engaged in Republican politics from his years in Little York and Red Dog. He continued these activities and alliances in San Diego through the late 1890s, nearly to the end of his life. He was elected chairman of the Republican County Committee in 1875 and was the Third Ward delegate to the Republican Convention in 1878. (Ephraim Morse, A. E. Horton, John Young, and J. B Levet were the Fourth Ward delegates that year.)

In the City Election of May 1878, W. A. Begole failed to be re-elected to a third term as a city trustee. He was defeated by another Republican, Arthur H. Julian (77 votes to 60). Julian was both a Fifth Street neighbor as well as a fellow tinsmith and hardware dealer. A letter to the editor on May 9 in the *San Diego Union* signed "Fair Play,"

W. A. Begole's tin shop and hardware store at 529 Fifth Street still stands in San Diego's Gaslamp District.
[TOP]: *Taken sometime after September 1878 when the San Diego Union reported completion of W. A. Begole's "new" brick building.*
[OPPOSITE PAGE]: *Taken in 2012 by the author. In 2016 the "Begole-Higgins" block was subjected to another renovation which has obscured the original architecture and its historical significance.*

argued for his re-election and described W. A.'s many virtues. This letter provides a glimpse into W. A. Begole's character through the ways his contemporary supporters saw him, and a glimpse of the contentiousness over railroad-related board action that colored the 1878 city election:

> W. A. Begole has surely performed his work faithfully and well, and won even from his opponents the title of "Old Honesty." He is an intelligent, fair-minded business man, and a strict economist. His success in his own private business is his sure recommendation and good evidence of his ability to manage the affairs of the public. From the outset he has never wavered in his devotion to the railroad interests of San Diego—never favored anything but the original Texas Pacific Railroad bill straight through to this bay—no compromise—has always been hopeful of our ultimate success, and never has spoken a disparaging word to dampen the hope of others. But this with the "new dealers" constitutes crime enough for any man's removal. They are determined if possible by every means foul and fair to clean out those faithful public servants, undo what they have done regards Railroad matters, defeat the will of the people and defraud our agents in Washington out of their just dues. The voters of the Third Ward have it in their power to say to these new dealers in politics, "You have gone far enough," and by re-electing Mr. Begole again, you assure for Trustee a man of sterling merit and have the Railroad business carried out in a sensible business-like manner. Do not fail to vote for Mr. Begole.[108]

"Fair Play"'s letter fails to explain why exactly W. A. lost the election to A. H. Julian. On the surface, it would seem that the two men would be more aligned than opposed and that Arthur Julian was not one of the "new dealers" that "Fair Play" describes. Arthur Julian was a Republican, an active affiliate in Masonic Lodge No. 35, a railroad promoter, and a vice president with W. A. Begole of the Republican-dominated

San Diego Chamber of Commerce. Adding credence to this impression, the *San Diego Union* in an editorial the next day praised election results and congratulated voters for staying the course. And two weeks later, Third Ward Republicans recommended both Begole and Julian as good potential delegates to the upcoming Republican County Convention, along with Simon Levi, Ephraim Morse, and three other good "new boys." In the delegates election, Begole was chosen, Julian was not.[109]

However, despite all these commonalities, Arthur H. Julian may have been among the critics of the city trustees' decision to issue a new round of railroad bonds to "carry out the agreement made in 1872 with Col. Thomas Scott." After all, Scott's railroad never materialized. Minutes from the city trustees' meetings from October 1877 suggest tension and disagreement around the trustees' actions. The minutes record that W. L. Williams refused to accept his election as city treasurer. The minutes also include the text of a brazen "warning," published in the *San Diego News* and other California newspapers, that declared the new city bonds illegal and void. The warning was signed by sixteen prominent San Diegans, including Jacob M. Julian,[110] a Democrat and publisher of the *San Diego News,* and Andrew Cassidy, former trustee and county supervisor. Several signers were Fifth Street businessmen, presumably from Ward 3. The minutes also include the text of a fight-back resolution, which was passed, accusing the signers of "collusion and preconcert with enemies of the Texas and Pacific Railway Company and of the City of San Diego," and initiating a lawsuit to recover damages. Begole and the Republican County Committee leadership had also been the subject of politically based criticism in the past by Democrat Jacob Julian when he was editor of the *World*.[111] Battles over railroad policies and city politics are too complex for this story to cover adequately; they are well described in texts by San Diego historians listed in the bibliography. Too, this story's focus on W. A. Begole regrettably prevents a deeper dive into the kin relationships, if any, between Republican merchant Arthur Julian, Democrat newspaperman Jacob Julian, Mike Julian (for whom the town of Julian was named), and the other families with the "Julian" surname who were living in San Diego at this time.

W. A.'s defeat at the 1878 polls appears not to have disturbed his alliances, appointments, activities, commitments to the city—or his vacation plans. The next week W. A. travelled to San Francisco to party at the Third Annual Reunion of the "Old Nevadans." There, his fellow pioneer miners elected him the San Diego representative to the Old Nevadans Corresponding Committee.[112] The party went on for several days. According to a lengthy article three years before on the front page of the *Sacramento Daily Record-Union*, the first reunion of the mining pioneers in May 1876 was even more of a doozie, many months in the making. The *Union* reported that several thousand "foothill miners gathered together on the old stomping ground to shake hands with yesterday," and that several thousand more pioneer miners were located across the continent and contacted.[113]

That fall, Begole was elected an officer and recording secretary of the San Diego Society of Natural History. In another area of his interest, the city trustees (including his election opponent Arthur Julian), appointed W. A. Begole, W. L. Williams, Lewis C. Gunn, David Felsenheld, and A. B. Hotchkiss to a National and International Convention in Chicago of merchants, manufacturers, and others interested in advancing foreign and reciprocal trade. More railroad boosting. W. A. was still enough of a public figure that when his loyal bird dog "Fannie" died from a "supposed" accidental poisoning two days before Christmas 1879, the *San Diego Union* ran a story about it.[114]

In the late 1870s, a "secret" San Diego Railroad Committee appointed Frank Kimball of National City to enter railroad negotiations on the East Coast. The San Diegans believed that titans Charles Crocker, Colis Huntington, Leland Stanford, and Mark Hopkins were manipulating policy to favor their Southern Pacific Railroad and strengthen its dominance. Kimball's extensive efforts this time finally achieved incorporation of the California Southern Railroad in October 1880. The contract involved his family's extensive land holdings in National City as well as a new publicly subscribed subsidy for the new railroad comprising cash, notes, and land. Several hundred subscribers raised $25,410, 17,355 acres, and 485 lots. W. A. Begole was among them; he contributed $50 and one lot.[115] Construction began immediately. The first rail was laid in June 1881, and by late August reached from National City to the foot of Fifth Street in New Town. The line reached Colton in August 1882.[116] (There would be, however, a donnybrook with the San Francisco titans over line crossing, which the Southern California Railroad won, and more before the rail connection was secured and open once and for all.)

Circling back to the bedfellows who were pushing San Diego's development, seven of the twelve elected members of the 1882 County Republican Central Committee were subscribers to the public subsidy for the California Southern Railroad. Members Begole, Capron, Cave, Harbison, Hubbell, Luce, and Simpson all kicked in comparably to the effort. Other Republican Central Committee members that year were Judge M. A. Luce (judge of the County Court, attorney and vice president of the California Southern Railroad), J. S. Harbison, J. H. Simpson (shipping agent), Dr. Daniel Cave (dentist), John G. Capron (merchant and member of Frank Kimball's "secret" committee to advance a railroad connection to San Diego bay), G.G. Bradt (insurance agent), C. C. Watson (California assemblyman from San Diego), Charles Hubbell (city treasurer, banker, farmer, railroad committee), E. E. Burgess, J. Murrieta, J. C. Hayes, and D. Burroughs (City Assessor and Otay Valley farmer).[117] W. A. Begole was appointed chair of the finance committee and was a delegate to the county convention as chairman of the committee on resolutions.

As the decade turned, with the depression subsiding and railroad news heating up, sleepy San Diego stepped with great promotional hoopla into the next big boom, invigorating W. A.'s real estate investments, business contracts, fraternal activities, and political efforts and complicating his personal life.

## *1881, Marriage. 1882, Divorce.*

It would seem, also at this time, that W. A. Begole, a fifty-seven-year-old bachelor with entrenched miner's habits who lived alone, must have been running a romance (or working a business match) with a slightly younger woman, Helen E. Hanford. They married on April 24, 1881, in the Presbyterian Church in San Diego. Presumably, the church affiliation was Helen's. The ceremony was performed by the Reverend Dodge, and official witnesses were Douglas Gunn's father, Lewis C. Gunn, and George Marston.[118] Whether there were other guests or whether the new Mrs. William Augustus Begole was part of a social circle that included W. A., Gunn, and Marston or whether she even knew Gunn and Marston, are unknown. Except for one pioneer picnic and a fireman's ball, there are no references in the newspaper records that link W. A. Begole to a social circle or to any church or leisure activities.

We know little about Helen Hanford, only that in 1880, from the Federal Census that: 1) she was living and "keeping house" in her unmarried son's household in the San Pasqual Valley; 2) her son's name was George White Butterfield; 3) George had registered to vote in the San Pasqual Valley in 1879; 4) George was born in Massachusetts when Helen was seventeen; 5) Helen was born in Vermont; and 6) George's wife's (Jessie Rickey) family's genealogical records claim that George was related somehow to the John W. Butterfield and Sons who operated the Butterfield Stage twenty years earlier.[119] We also know that Helen Hanford must have had the financial means to unload a rogue husband.

The Begole–Hanford marriage bloomed, wilted, and died in about eighteen months. It's unclear if the couple ever lived together; there was no residential directory for San Diego City for 1881–1882, the year they were married. By August 1882, the couple was suing each other over loans. He purchased from her a property in Horton's Addition, on Sixteenth Street, for $1,100 in late August; she filed her divorce petition at the end of September. By that November, they were divorced, and Helen Hanford had resumed her former name. We learn from public court records only that she accused him of adultery with a lady of the night or maybe several in "The Palace" on Sixth Street, presumably a bordello around the corner from his business on Fifth Street. Beyond Helen's statement, the court records are silent. There is no respondent's statement or testimony in the court file. W. A. did not show up for the hearing.

Without a record of W. A.'s response to Helen's accusations, or diaries or letters of his or hers, or court testimony of any kind, it's impossible to know with certainty what really happened between them. Maybe W. A. did carry his frontier habits into the marriage and his behavior was as scandalous as it appears. If this was the case, one would imagine that court records would reveal more of a scuffle and that W. A.'s reputation among San Diego's hoi polloi would have suffered much more than the record suggests. But at least according to the newspapers, he seems not to have been ostracized in any realm of his life. Rather, W. A. Begole was busier and more deeply involved in political and civic life than ever in these years that flanked the arrival (at last!) of the California Southern Railroad in 1885.

Another plausible interpretation of the same facts is that filing for divorce on the grounds of W. A. Begole's alleged adultery was the fastest, easiest way for the couple to dissolve a marriage that suited neither spouse. Divorce was difficult in the 1880s. (In California, grounds for divorce were adultery, extreme cruelty, willful desertion or neglect for one year, habitual intemperance for one year, or conviction of felony.[120]) Perhaps adultery, especially at this time, was the least offensive choice to the reputation of a popular civic leader. There is some circumstantial evidence for this.

Other than the litigation over money and property and the property transfer, which were all quickly resolved and completed during the summer before Helen's September 1882 filing, there are no traces of contention, no counter accusations or suggestions by actions or statements that either party was emotionally upset by the divorce. Further, the witnesses for Helen Begole appear to be W. A.'s business associates rather than personal affiliations of hers. Witness Harry Piley was a Customs House officer.[121] The second witness, "Marion Bowers," is quite likely James Marion Bowers, a brother of W. A. Begole's longtime Masonic brother, the prominent and influential US Senator William Wallace Bowers.[122] Bowers' wife, Lucy Horton Bowers, was Alonzo Horton's sister. J. M. Bowers appears in the San Diego press at the time as a buyer-seller of real estate,[123] who sat on at least one civic board with George Marston and the other city elite. W. W. Bowers was also W. A.'s business associate, friend and, twenty years later, his pallbearer.

We'll never know the true story behind the salacious facts. But the Begole divorce in 1882 certainly appears to have been a non-event among these friends and city movers, as the next chapter details. Both Helen and W. A. Begole remained in San Diego, where Helen E. Hanford died several years later in her son's home.

# Chapter Six

## Early 1880s: Run-Up to San Diego's Late '80s Boom-a-Rama

**I**N THE YEARS leading up to the railroad's arrival, W. A. Begole travelled frequently between San Diego, Los Angeles, and San Diego, sometimes alone and sometimes with business associates Douglas Gunn and Philip Morse. When he was not a passenger steaming on the *Orizaba*, the *Ancon*, or the *Queen of the Pacific* between San Diego, Los Angeles, and San Francisco, he was shipping or receiving materials and products. He was also doing work for the city; his bills to the city trustees were recorded regularly in the minutes and in newspaper accounts of these meetings.

In March 1882, the Masons opened their new Masonic Building at Sixth and H Streets. W. A. built the time capsule that contained three daily papers and other mementoes that was placed in the cornerstone of the new building. He was also elected to the board of directors and began serving as secretary of the new Masonic Association, a position he held for many more years.[124]

The month of September 1882, when Helen filed for divorce, was crammed both with fraternal and political projects. For the founding

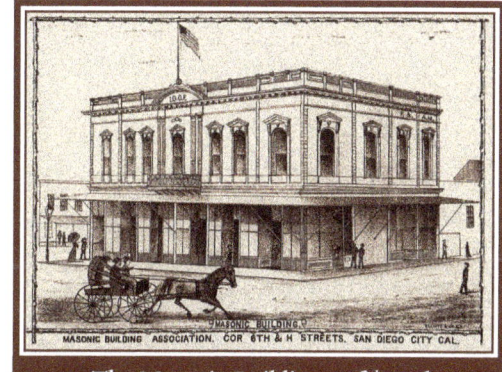

*The Masonic Building at 6th and H Streets was around the corner from W. A.'s tin shop at 529 Fifth.*

of the Royal Arch Masons No. 61, W. A. was elected high priest and treasurer of the new chapter and was also in charge of outfitting and dressing up the lodge rooms.[125] There were also a slew of Republican initiatives leading up to and including the Republican county convention, for which W. A. played a number of different roles. San Diegan Republicans formed a "Young Men's Republicans Club" to the loud guffaws of most of the members who "had crossed the shady side of life and were basking in the sunshine of antiquity."[126] From the small crowd of usual suspects, most of who were also Masonic Lodge No. 35 affiliates, W. A. was appointed to the finance committee. At the Republican county convention, W. A. was the chairman on resolutions and was appointed both to the county Republican Central Committee and to the senator nominating committee that would, with its San Bernardino counterpart, nominate their joint Republican candidate for the California Senate.[127]

At the beginning of October, W. A.'s friend and fellow Mason, Captain Nelson Olds, died. Brothers W. A. Begole, William Wallace Bowers, W. W. Stewart, A. H. Julian, E. W. Bushyhead, and A. Stephens were pallbearers.[128] Days later, W. A. was appointed an election inspector for Ward 3 by the San Diego Board of Supervisors.[129] Nine days later, another San Diego notable, Judge McNealy, heard and granted the Begole divorce.[130]

## *Cousin Josiah William Begole Elected Michigan Governor*

A week after the divorce was granted, on November 7, 1882, W. A's first cousin, Josiah William Begole of Flint, Michigan, was elected Michigan Governor as the Fusion Party candidate. Josiah had been involved in city and state politics for some time: Flint City Council member, state senator (1870–1871), delegate to the Republican National Convention (1872), and member of the US Congress (1873–1875). A Flint pioneer, lumberman, and banker, Josiah Begole was also a founder of Flint Water and Gas Works, a vice president of Citizens and Commercial Savings Bank in Flint, and owner of Flint Wagon Works, manufacturer of wagons. As the nineteenth century turned to the twentieth, Flint Wagon Works, following the invention of the combustion engine and under the tutelage of Josiah's son, Charles Myron Begole, evolved into the Chevrolet and Buick Motor companies.[131] W. A. and his older cousin, Josiah, grew up together in the wilderness of Mount Morris, New York, sons of brothers. Josiah visited W. A. in San Diego several times before and after his tenure as governor.[132]

*W. A. Begole's tin roofs adorned* [TOP]: *The Florence Hotel (photo c. 1887), owned by W. W. Bowers, who was Alonzo Horton's brother-in-law, and* [BOTTOM]: *San Diego's First National Bank (photo c. 1883).*

During the next few years between business trips, W. A. Begole built the tin roofs on W. W. Bowers' new showplace, the Florence Hotel, and the new First National and Commercial Bank buildings. He was also appointed regularly to the grand jury pool by the county board of supervisors and joined the efforts of San Diego Republicans to elect Blaine and Logan.

## 1885: Through Train from San Diego to the Continent

In November 1885, the last spike was driven and the first through train departed San Diego, ending thirty years of railroad frustrations and launching the grand land boom of the late 1880s. The railroad and the public relations and hype that came with it pulled throngs of tourists, speculators and immigrants to San Diego County. Frederick G. Hoyt, in his analysis of the 1880s boom, quotes historian Glenn S. Dumke, who wrote, "A basic cause of the boom of the 1880s was the extensive advertising and publicity campaign which carried information about southern California to all parts of the world."[133] It was time to cash in.

Again, fortunes were to be made and lost by "Sixty-Niner" pioneers who had toughed out the depressions and droughts, and toiled for a few decades to realize the windfall promised in the 1860s by Horton's big-city vision, and by newcomers as well.

Hoyt dissects the article, "SAN DIEGO: The Brilliant, Booming Metropolis of the Extreme Southwest," that appeared on June 25, 1887 in the Chicago daily *Inter Ocean*, its authorship attributed only to the initials "C. A." Hoyt supposes that the story was a puff piece commissioned by the San Diego Chamber of Commerce and financed by city "boosters" whose contribution amounts were reflected in the varied sizes of the spiels about their businesses. Hoyt writes that realtors and developers dominated the featured businesses and that "pushing," whatever it entailed, was an attribute highly praised in San Diego in 1887, as in "a pushing, wide awake real estate firm" and "one of the pushing firms who are hoping to settle Southern California." "Capitalists" also received C. A.'s admiration.[134]

Oddly, the three featured firms that received such high praise from "C. A." are not listed in the official 1886–1887 San Diego City Directory. Perhaps the sponsors of this effort in the Chicago press were not the Chamber old guard, after all?[135] Wilmer Shields points out that the number of realtors listed in the San Diego City Directory exploded from 46 in 1886–1887 to 136 in 1887–1888.[136]

Pourade also attributes the boom that followed the completion of the rail link to hyperbolic promotion of Southern California by the railroads themselves, land speculators, and other boosters seeking to enrich themselves. "By mid-1886 several thousand persons were arriving in San Diego monthly by train and ship. Seeking speculative markets, outside capital reached into the County. Land speculators boarded incoming trains at Oceanside, offering land in that area 'at bargain prices,' or at anyplace else."[137] He writes enticingly about San Diego's boom times in *The Glory Years*:

> The two years that began in 1886 and ended in 1888 were the most gaudy, wicked and exciting in San Diego's history. The boomers and gamblers had followed the speculators to San Diego and now came the entertainers and the criminals. It was San Francisco of the Gold Rush all over again.[138]

# Chapter Seven

## 1886: W. A.'s Life Shift at 60

**T**HE RAILROAD CONNECTION went north from National City through San Diego, Oceanside, Fallbrook, Temecula, Murrieta, Perris, and Lake Elsinore and linked San Diego with the transcontinental system in Colton near the Cajon Pass.[139] In 1885, "Murrieta's train depot was finished and a town site began to grow around the nucleus of the depot; pioneer families are drawn by advertisements of land for as little as $5 an acre. In that year, a 50' × 140' lot in the town site sold from $20 to $75."[140]

In July 1886, W. A. Begole sold the north half of his double lot on Fifth Street for $5,000,[141] nearly fifteen times what he paid in 1869 for the entire property, retaining for himself the south lot where his brick tin shop was located. In November, he sold another property. In 1886, 1888, and again in 1890, he registered to vote in Murrieta, then a backcountry burg on the rail line 75 miles north of New Town San Diego. He registered his occupation as "merchant"—not "tinsmith."[142] (Helen Hanford, formerly Begole, had died in May 1886. There is no mention of their marriage in her funeral notice.[143])

Judging from the few records that exist, W. A. Begole's Murrieta sojourn was tentative and short-lived. W. A. made no Murrieta property purchases during the time he was supposed to have been a Murrieta merchant. Although W. A.'s lack of a San Diego advertisement and listing in Maxwell's San Diego City Directory for 1887–1888 is, on one hand, additional evidence for his absence from San Diego that year, on the other hand, he was not listed in Murrieta either, or anywhere in

San Diego County. And, although W. A. served as Master of San Diego Masonic Lodge No. 35 in 1885, and as high priest of the San Diego Royal Arch Masons Chapter No. 61 in 1883, 1884, 1886, and 1888, he did not serve either in 1867.

It seems out of character for W. A., a consistent advertiser since his earliest days in Red Dog, to start a new merchandising venture without advertising. Perhaps W. A. profited from the boom in ways we can't see in the records, and perhaps he was an investor behind the scenes rather than on the face of the merchant operation. We would expect his new venture to be promoted similarly to the puff paragraph that accompanied W. A.'s display advertisement in the 1886–1887 San Diego City Directory, the way he'd promoted his business for many years:

> **W. A. Begole keeps a very extensive stock of hardware, stoves, ranges and every article usually found in first class establishments of any kind. Mr. Begole also conducts an excellent tin shop in connection with his business, and deals largely in bath tubs, water and wall pipe, etc. See advertisement on another page.**[144]

His business advertising ceased in 1886.

W. A.'s reduced public profile in 1887 suggests that his life changed quite fundamentally at this time. Beyond his lack of business advertising, newspaper articles and records of his business travels and shipments, even his fraternal and political activities also seem diminished in comparison to other years. Except for his jury service on a murder trial in November 1887,[145] we don't find much about W. A. in San Diego newspapers after July 1886 when he represented Fifth Street property owners in front of the city trustees in a neighborhood dust-up with the San Diego Street Railroad Company.[146] He resurfaces in late summer of 1888, after the boom had busted and when Republican Club activities picked up in anticipation of the presidential election. In August 1888, W. A. was elected first vice-president of the Third Ward Republicans Presidential Election Committee to support Benjamin Harrison and Levi Morton,[147] and he was also appointed election judge for the Third Precinct of the Third Ward by the San Diego Board of Supervisors.[148]

*Fifth Street, San Diego, built-out and bustling in 1888, looking south from Broadway*

## 1888: W. A. Begole and the New City Charter Elections

In November 1888, W. A. was elected (with longtime cohorts Douglas Gunn, Philip Morse, N. H. Conklin, M. A. Luce, Ephraim Morse, D. Cave, Charles Hubbell, and others) to a commission of fifteen "freeholders" to "make the new City Charter."[149] Clearly prominent in San Diego civic and political circles, W. A. Begole was also among the glitterati when they entertained Senator and Mrs. Leland Stanford for luncheon at the Hotel Del Coronado that December; a few of the others were Douglas Gunn, Judge Luce, Frank Kimball, T. S. Van Dyke, W. W. Stewart, E. W. Bushyhead, George Hazzard, and H. C. Nash.[150]

The new San Diego City Charter was adopted on March 2, 1889, and approved by the State Legislature on March 16. According to the new charter, the city would be run by an elected mayor and a "common council" comprising a nine-member Board of Aldermen and an eighteen-member Board of Delegates. The city election took place on April 2, 1889, with the leadership of the Republican Party in the city so challenged that the party split into two warring factions. William Smythe's history delves a bit into this, another San Diego story that is too complex to explain here. Smythe writes:

> The campaign presented many features of interest. There were two tickets in the field, one called the Straight Republican, headed by John R. Berry (editor of the Union), and the other called the Citizens Non-Partisan ticket, headed by Douglas Gunn. Both these candidates were Republicans and there was no Democratic ticket. The real issue of the campaign was between 'the Gallaghers'—carpetbaggers from San Francisco who came during the boom and obtained control of the Republican organization in city and county—and the older citizens of San Diego. It was charged that these 'Gallaghers' were for the most part Democrats before coming to San Diego. They had succeeded in electing a few of their candidates the year before, including the Superior Court Judge. The Union supported Berry, but the other papers were for Gunn, and party lines were much broken up.[151]

W. W. Bowers--a Republican leader, Alonzo Horton's brother-in-law, and a San Diego "old timer"—spoke in favor of the Citizens ticket that was headed by candidate for mayor Douglas Gunn, George Marston's brother-in-law. Douglas Gunn and W. A. Begole ran not on the Republican ticket but on the Citizens ticket for mayor and alderman, respectively. Both were elected with most of the Citizens' candidates in 1889.

W. A. Begole resurfaced in *Monteith's Directory of San Diego and Vicinity for 1889–1890*, touted by the publisher John C. Monteith as "the most thorough and complete canvas [sic] ever made in this city."[152] W. A. Begole appeared in this directory as a "capitalist" living at 529 Fifth Street. However, 529 Fifth Street was no longer W. A.'s tin shop. In Monteith's 1889–1890 Directory, the old tin shop address belonged to the Santa Clara Lodging House. The directory deadline must have been after the April 1889 election. Monteith's list of city officials showed Douglas Gunn as mayor and W. A. Begole as alderman.

## *The New Regime: Stewardship and Non-Partisanship*

On May 8, 1889, San Diego's first elected mayor, Douglas Gunn, and separate legislative bodies of aldermen and delegates launched the new City Charter and the new organization of the city with an enormous public meeting. The lengthy article covering it in the *San Diego Weekly Union* began:

> It was like the modern railway show, both under the same stretch of canvas—the Board of Aldermen as the menagerie, and the delegates as the grand three-ring circus. At any rate the crowd was there. Some passed the door and others slipped under the tent. The general curiosity to see the city machinery put into operation under the new charter was great, and long before either body was ready to convene a crowd had gathered at City Hall and was standing about the corridors, halls and in the council chamber. Mayor Gunn was quickly surrounded as soon as he made his appearance and an effort was made to learn from him the drift of events in certain directions. The new mayor was as calm and self-possessed as ever. He bore his new dignity becomingly, and was as skillful as of old in not committing himself about the chances of the candidates.[153]

The aldermen and delegates convened to elect their leader. The aldermen met in a small room with barely enough seating for themselves —and immediately locked the door to keep the public out. Wise minds prevailed, however, and they unlocked the door. As the first business of their first meeting, "W. A. Begole was quickly persuaded to permit of the honor (of temporary chairmanship) being thrust upon him. He took a cane-bottomed office chair in nowise different or more elevated than the rest, and quietly stroking his long whiskers stated that he supposed the first thing necessary was the election of a permanent chairman. There was a low growl in anticipation of this." What was anticipated was a floor battle between Aldermen Levi and Fisher, both of whom very much wanted the job. After eleven ballots, with W. A.'s name thrown into the hat on the second, the group evidently compromised, electing neither Levi nor Fischer, but H. T. Christian. After the vote, W. A. "released his temporary authority and the cane bottomed chair, which, out of consideration of the dignity of the Chairmanship, had been placed within aiming distance to the only cuspidor in the room."[154]

With leadership of the aldermen and delegates determined, the crowd reassembled to hear Mayor Douglas Gunn speak. In a lengthy statement that explained what the non-partisans had been up to for the preceding few years and also set forth their mission and detailed agenda, Gunn announced a significant commitment from the new regime to stewardship and non-partisanship:

> The movement of the citizens of San Diego, which has given us the recent significant decisions at the ballot box, is very much more than a transient manifestation of discontent with the preceding administration of city affairs. It is a result of a belief that had been steadily growing in the public mind until it had become a fixed conviction that we must reform the municipal constitution before we could effectively reform the municipal administration. It was obvious at the outset that such a consummation could only be reached through the concurrent action of all citizens who were convinced of its necessity without regard to their difference of opinion upon questions of party politics. The movement was therefore necessarily non-partisan in its organization and the attainment of its primary object was logically followed by the election of non-partisan officers to carry the provisions of the new instrument of government into practical operation. It will undoubtedly continue to manifest itself in future elections.
>
> A city is essentially a corporation organized to secure certain public benefits and doing business upon the capital represented by its assessment roll, in which every taxpayer is a shareholder and the city officers are the directors chosen to carry on its affairs for the common advantage. The shareholders in

other corporations do not concern themselves about the political views of their trustees so long as the trust is profitably and honestly managed; and the fact that this is a public corporation affords no reason for a departure from the commonsense rules of private business.

In the election which has placed the government of this city in our hands, upon a distinct presentation of the issue the people very plainly declared against the application of any political test, and demanded that the business of the city should be conducted upon strictly business principles. The obligation resting upon us as the servants of the people is manifest.[155]

After Gunn finished, W. A. Begole "offered a motion that a vote of thanks be tendered to Mayor Gunn expressing the gratification of the board for the elaborate manner in which [Gunn] had set out the needs of the city and its financial condition." Mayor Gunn, younger by fifteen years than W. A. Begole, was also a New Town "Sixty-Niner," a fellow Mason, and longtime associate. W. A. likely had been part of the "revolution" in San Diego's city government and in setting its new agenda.

W. A.'s committee assignments during his term as alderman reflect his interest, experience, and expertise in "the works" of things: sewers, health, and morals; water and fire; public buildings and lighting; and police. That the Sewers and Health Committee also threw "morals" into the mix adds an interesting twist to the idea of "expertise" since W. A. had been accused of adultery with *"une fille de joie"* a few years before. (This was a new time and place, though. Perhaps W. A.'s interest in morals and police demonstrated a desire to address the decline of his immediate neighborhood. During the 1880s boom, the Lower Fifth neighborhood had attracted a tough new crowd of vice peddlers. As early as 1881, there were a few buildings on Lower Fifth known as "Stingaree Row" or "Stingaree Block." In 1888, there were at least 120 "bawdy houses" in the city; it was unsafe for anyone to walk at night below Market, and no "decent" San Diego lady would venture there at any time.[156])

As Mayor Gunn's launch statement had predicted, the next two years were packed with issues of considerable significance to the city. W. A. Begole was a steady and conservative presence at meetings of the Board of Aldermen. William Ellsworth Smythe writes, "Between the end of the boom and the summer of 1891, many of the most important permanent public and private improvements in San Diego were completed."[157] More than $10 million was invested by Smythe's account on projects, including the rebuilding of the court house; the laying of several miles of street pavement; the extension of the electric railway to University Heights, and of the San Diego, Cuyamaca, and Eastern Railway to El Cajon; and the completion and opening of the Hotel Del Coronado. The flume was completed and began to deliver water to the city. Schoolhouses and churches were built. The population of the city had grown slowly out of the bust to about 17,000 by the 1890 Federal Census, about six times what it had been at the beginning of the 1880s. Among this batch of post-boom newcomers was John D. Spreckles, who would make all the difference to San Diego.

Once W. A. Begole's term as alderman was finished—the new city charter launched, professional police and fire departments established, administrative posts filled, committees created and functioning—he did not seek a second term. Neither did Gunn, whom historian Richard Crawford calls an "unsung pioneer," seek a second term as mayor. W. A.'s friend was found dead in his office on November 21, 1891. Gunn had invested heavily in San Diego real estate and promoting the city. Just prior to leading the effort to reorganize the city, Gunn created and published the lavishly photographed tome *Picturesque San Diego* and donated 2,000 copies to the San Diego Chamber of Commerce; he resigned as president of the Chamber in order to assume his elected role as mayor in 1889. Gunn lost heavily in the crash of 1888, was compelled to borrow at ruinous interest rates, and never recouped his fortunes. He died just days before this note was due.[158] Gunn's obituary notes that "He was survived by his elderly parents; his brother Chester Gunn, a county supervisor; and his sister Anna Lee Gunn, who was married to businessman George W. Marston."[159] The reader will recall that Gunn's father, Lewis C. Gunn, and brother-in-law, George Marston, were the witnesses at W. A's wedding in 1881.

# Chapter Eight

## 1890s: W. A.'s Last Decade — Back to Mining, Masonic Activities, and Civic Duties

**DOUGLAS GUNN WAS** not alone in suffering devastating financial losses during the decade that Elizabeth MacPhail calls "The Not-So-Gay Nineties, 1890–1899".[160] The Gilded Age ended across the United States with the financial panic of 1893. In San Diego, tough financial times came early; much of the decade between 1890 and 1900 was difficult for many. Crash-related debt, exorbitant interest rates, and local bank failures, beginning with the failure of the California National Bank in 1891, wiped out the investments and savings of hundreds of San Diegans and restrained investment in the immediate future. Of the eight banks in San Diego in 1889, five would fail in the early1890s. Even gambler and saloon owner Wyatt Earp left town for greener pastures.

Many of W. A.'s cohorts who rode the booms and busts of the 1870s and 1880s experienced tough times after the 1888 crash. It's true that W. A. had no fancy properties or other acquisitions to sustain. He was a bachelor with no wife to squire about town, no extravagant lifestyle, no elegant transportation or wardrobe requirements, and no children to support or educate. He himself lived alone over the store at 529 Fifth Street for his entire San Diego life, presumably simply, even as the Lower Fifth neighborhood degenerated in the late 1890s into a glut of saloons, gambling halls, and whorehouses. By 1897, as per that year's City and County Directory,[161] 529 Fifth Street had become the Santa Clara Lodging House and was also the listed address of W. A.'s residence.

Whether W. A. Begole slipped into financial embarrassment or even ruin during the last decade of his life is unclear in public records but is certainly suggested. Grantee and grantor records in the San Diego County Assessor's office show that W. A. sold six properties between 1886 and 1894, four after 1891 when tight times began, and only one for more than $1,000. Especially poignant and somewhat mysterious is the last transaction in 1894, which transfers his brick building and property at 529 Fifth Street to real estate agent J. A. P. Vauclain for the token amount of $5. Vauclain sold the property two days later for $6,000 to Martine Chick, a gun dealer.

At the same time, in the early 1890s, W. A. evidently had funds to invest in mining partnerships in Pine Valley from which he and his partners seem to have realized a satisfying return. In July 1893, the *San Diego Weekly Union* in its "Local Intelligence" column reported, "another shipment" of bullion worth about $4,000 arrived Friday from the Free Coinage Mine on Indian Creek in the Pine Valley district, owned by the Hawkes brothers, J. A. Heath, and W. A. Begole. The shaft is only twenty-five feet in depth, and the mine promises to do a rare thing—pay from the grassroots down."[162] A second mine in the same area, the Double Standard Mine, a "mine of phenomenal yield" owned by D. F. and E. Hawkes, W. A. Begole and others, hyped by D. F. Hawkes a year later: "Specimens of the rock brought in showed remarkable richness. Probably there was never rock discovered in Southern California that was any richer or as rich as this."[163] Reports of "a good clean-up" from the Free Coinage appeared again in May 1896.[164]

In an 1896 swan-song foray into San Diego City politics (this time high-stakes water politics), W. A. Begole, as a former member of the City Alderman Water and Fire Committee, was rallied to join forces —with 99 other of the influential old guard, many of them "retired" (to include D. C. Reed, Ed Bushyhead, S. W. Craigue, J. S. Harbison, G. G. Bradt, and others)—as a vice-president of the 100-member "Municipal Ownership Club." Their mission was to defeat a city partnership with John D. Spreckles' private Mountain Water Company and the $1.5 million city bond issue to support it and to secure municipal ownership of San Diego's water system. After a messy battle that reached into the mayoral elections, the winner was Spreckles, who made expeditious use of his ownership of the *San Diego Union*.[165]

W. A. also continued his affiliations with Masonic Lodge No. 35, Royal Arch Masons No. 61 and Commandery No. 25 Knights Templar throughout the decade, serving in a continuing string of leadership roles for all three. W. A. took a "business" trip in October 1897 on the Santa Fe Railroad to Burlingame, Kansas,[166] most likely to visit his brother, Joshua Begole, who lived there. In December, he was elected marshal of Lodge No. 35, where he had served six terms as master, and he was re-elected treasurer of Royal Arch Masons No. 61.[167] W. A. was a member of a contingent from Lodge No. 35 that travelled to Escondido in the fall of 1898 for a presentation to the local Masons.[168] A month later, he served as pallbearer for his old friend and Masonic brother, Chalmers Scott, with Judge McNealy, George Fuller, E. E. Shaffer, and S. W. Craigue.

## ANNUAL MEETING.

The regular annual meeting of the stockholders of the Masonic Building association will be held at the Masonic hall, corner H and Sixth streets, on Monday, March 5, 1900, at 7 o'clock p.m. for the purpose of electing directors for the ensuing year, and for the transaction of such other business as may be presented at the hour of meeting.
W. A. BEGOLE, President.
W. W. STEWART, Sec'y.
San Diego, Feb. 23, 1900.

*W. A. Begole remained president of the Masonic Building Association until the last year of his life, when W. W. Stewart took over. This meeting notice appeared in March 1900.[170]*

In May 1899 W. A. was elected recorder and in 1900 treasurer of Commandery No. 25.[169] He continued to be appointed reliably year after year by the San Diego County Supervisors to the pool of possible grand jurors and as an election judge in the Third Ward. He was president of the Masonic Building Association at least through the spring of 1900.

For at least the first year of the final two years of his life, W. A. Begole was a "boarder" in the home of Mrs. Caroline S. Chandler, widow of Henry L. Chandler, the proprietor of the Star Restaurant on Fifth

Street. Henry and Caroline Chandler were likely W. A.'s longtime friends. Beginning in the early 1880s, when the Chandlers first came to San Diego,[171] their Star Restaurant and residence above it shared the same block on Fifth Street with W. A.'s tin shop. (It may even have been next door to the tin shop. Records specify the block and not the street number.) Mrs. Chandler was also a beneficiary of the will that W. A. Begole wrote in 1895, six years before his death. She did not live to benefit from W. A.'s will, and she is buried within fifteen feet of him in the Masonic Division of the Mount Hope Cemetery.

Until the summer of 1900, news articles and notices show an active W. A. Begole, travelling and engaged in business activities, and leading his Masonic groups. On July 25, 1900, a brief item in the *Evening Tribune* reported that W. A. was "seriously ill in his rooms at Third and F from a stroke of apoplexy."[172] W. A.'s friend and landlord at 1214 F Street, Caroline S. Chandler, died just a month after W. A.'s stroke, and there are no more news items until his death thirteen months later. His obituary does not mention where he lived when he died.

William Augustus Begole died on September 1, 1901 at 4 o'clock in the afternoon. He was seventy-four years old. Coverage of his death begins with an obituary the following day in the *San Diego Union* and the *Evening Tribune*. Remembered by the *Union* as a devoted Mason, W. A.'s longtime service to the city—as city trustee, co-author of the City Charter, and Alderman elected to the "non-partisan" transition team—had already been forgotten.

> The death of W. A. Begole, one of the best known of the pioneers of San Diego, occurred yesterday afternoon at 4 o'clock of neuralgia of the heart. Mr. Begole was 74 years of age and was one of the first of the white men to cross the continent in 1849. He came to this city 33 years ago and for a great many years was in business here being known as the leading hardware merchant and plumber of the city. He was a leader in the Masonic circles for years and many of the Masons of San Diego can look back to the evening when W. A. Begole helped initiate them into the order. He was master of the San Diego Lodge

No. 35 for six terms, which is more than can be said of any Mason in Southern California with probably one exception. He succeeded himself for five years from 1871 to 1875, and ten years after retiring from the master's chair he was again elected and served during 1885. In business Mr. Begole was very conscientious and scrupulously honest in all his transactions, and it is doubtful if there is a man in the city who was held in higher regard than was the man who passed away, not unexpectedly, last night. Mr. Begole has no relatives living unless it be that death has not yet called ex-Governor Begole of Michigan, who was a brother of the deceased.

The San Diego Lodge No. 35 was his wife and family for he devoted many years and much energy to its up-building. It is understood that he has left a will and that the Master of San Diego Lodge who happens to be Sam F. Smith, is named as its executor. The arrangements for the funeral have not been made but it will be conducted by the Masons probably on Tuesday afternoon.

As Mr. Begole was known so far and wide as a Mason, and as the entire membership in the order hereabouts knew and respected the deceased, it is easy to guess that the funeral will show the largest turnout of Masons that the city has ever known.[173]

As the *Union* predicted, W. A. Begole's funeral was indeed a "touching expression of esteem which was felt by all the people of the city." More than 200 Masonic Sir Knights and Brothers turned out in full fraternal regalia on September 5, 1901, to honor their oldest member. Services were held in the Masonic temple and at the grave. Pallbearers W. W. Stewart, W. W. Bowers, Ed Bushyhead, Simon Levi, Ed Westcott, and Warren Hackett were friends and companions for years of the deceased. Two hundred Masons marched in slow and solemn step behind the casket up H Street. After one of the largest Masonic funerals in the history of the city, William Augustus Begole was buried in the Masonic Cemetery at Mount Hope.[174]

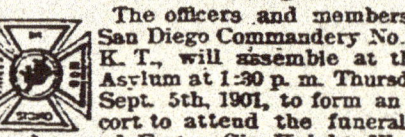

These notices calling his Masonic brothers for W. A. Begole's funeral appeared in the San Diego Union on September 5, 1901.[175]

W. A. Begole specified in his will that his gravestone be a monument of granite "not exceeding $250." He left four shares of Masonic Building stock to cover the costs of the funeral, granite marker, and care of the grave for five years. One hundred and fifteen years later, in the fall of 2016, the stone was restored by Thomas Patty, San Diego Grave Groomers.

Fifth Street, San Diego Pictured Across Time.
[Top]: *1869*, W. A. B. arrives in San Diego
[Middle]: *1888*, W. A. B. participates in writing the New San Diego City Charter
[Bottom]: *1901*, W. A. B. dies in September

# Appreciations and Acknowledgements

I want to thank San Diego historian Ellen Sweet (and friend of archeologist Bob Begole through her husband, Melvin) for inspiring this project, as well as the historians and genealogists who helped me locate, dig into, and make sense of the records: Jane Kenealy and Carol Myers, San Diego History Center; David Allen Lambert, Chief Genealogist, New England Historical Genealogical Society, Boston, Massachusetts; Peter Steelquist, San Diego Genealogical Society; John Goodloe, San Diego Masonic Lodge No. 35 F. & A.M.; Diane Brown, Nevada County Historical Society, Nevada City, California; San Diego historian Richard Crawford, California Room, San Diego Library; Nevada County historian David A. Comstock, Comstock-Bonanza Press, Santa Rosa, California, whose books and digitized biographical and newspaper digests of Nevada County are unique treasures; Jerry Brady, San Pedro, California, whose annual tour of Red Dog is publicized on the internet and led me to other sites and new revelations; my cousin by marriage, genealogist and family historian supreme, Ellen Gerwitz, Rochester, New York; historians Bob Fout, Frederick, Maryland, Jean Conte, Hagerstown, Maryland, and Dale Ladd, Flint, Michigan, whose research into the Begole and Bowles families in Maryland and Michigan has been invaluable; and Bruce and Alana Coons, Save our Heritage Organisation, San Diego, whose acquisition in 2013 and restoration in 2016 of "Little Slogan," W. A.'s "party cannon," makes the telling of this story right now especially timely.

I will be forever grateful, too, to my siblings, Lee and Bob Montgomery, my husband Jon, and my besties Ann Quinley, Maureen Convery, Melany Runyan, Rich Rudolf, and Suzanne Ward for their generosity and endurance in listening equally patiently to the details —picayune and monumental—of my OMG discoveries for the last five years. Their engagement with me on this journey has provided encouragement and such good company!

# Endnotes

## 2016 Restoration of Little Slogan

1) Fabert, Wayne M. and Ann Kantor. "San Diego's Centennial Celebration: A Pictorial Essay," Journal of San Diego History, Summer 1976, Vol 22, No.3.
2) San Diego Union Tribune, 'Little Slogan: Ownership of the Small Cannon Effectually Settled."

## Preface

3) Pourade, Richard F. *The History of San Diego: The Glory Years*, 137.
4) W. A.'s first cousin Josiah Begole (1815–1896) was a Flint, Michigan pioneer and Michigan Governor (1882–1884); Josiah's son, Charles Myron Begole, turned the family wagon business into the Buick and Chevrolet car companies. W. A.'s second cousin, Augustus William Begole (1837–1893), was a miner and pioneer founder of Ouray, Colorado; his nephew George Davis Begole became the Mayor of Denver. Another second cousin, Charles Dorrance Begole (1836–1890), was a miner and pioneer founder of Lone Pine, CA, and one of the three Anglo settlers of Lone Pine who first climbed Mount Whitney together in 1873.

## W. A. Begole Obituary

5) "Crossed the Plains with Donner Party." *San Francisco Call*, September 3, 1901

## Chapter One

6) *The Weekly Union*, Vol. 3, p. 2, San Diego, CA. September 9, 1869.
7) San Diego County Grantee Records, Book 6, p. 205. Lot D of Block 96 in Horton's Addition.
8) Andrew J. Russell (1830–1902), photographer, National Park Service, http://www.nps.gov/gosp/index.htm

9) San Diego County Grantee Records, Book 8, p. 277. Lot B of Block 123, Horton's Addition.
10) Koschmann, A. H. and M. H Bergendahl. "Principal Gold-Producing Districts of the United States."
11) MacPhail, Elizabeth C. *The Story of New San Diego and its Founder Alonzo E. Horton*, 14.
12) Steigler, Ione, Stephen Van Wormer, and Susan Walter. *Uptown Historic Context and Oral History Report*.
13) "Crossed the Plains with Donner Party." *San Francisco Call*, September 3, 1901
14) Stewart, George R. *The California Trail*, 301.
15) DeVoto, Bernard. *The Year of Decision 1846*.
16) Strauss, William and Neil Howe. *Generations: The History of America's Future, 1584–2069*, 206–227.

## Chapter Two

17) "Journal of the Committee of Observation of Frederick County, September 12, 1775—October 24, 1776," 52.
18) First Census of the United States, 1790.
19) Turner, Orasmus. *History of the Pioneer Settlement of Phelps and Gorham's Purchases and Morris Reserve*. Rochester, 551.
20) Ibid.
21) McMaster, Guy Humphrey. *History of the Settlement of Steuben County, New York, Including Notices of the Old Pioneer Settlers and Their Adventures*.
22) Benjamin Begole married second Maria Ewart (1810–1883). There were no children of this marriage.
23) Philo Begole is the author's great-great grandfather. Philo's son, Frederick Hurlburt Begole, visited San Diego City Father William Augustus Begole in San Diego when he was the Mayor of Marquette, Michigan.
24) Smith, James H. and Cale, Hume H. *History of Livingston County, New York, with Illustrations and Biographical Sketches, Some of Its Prominent Men and Pioneers*, 283–302.
25) Boston: Biographical Review Publishing Company. *Biographical*

26) Boston: Biographical Review Publishing Company. *Biographical Review; This volume contains biographical sketches of leading citizens of Livingston and Wyoming Counties, New York.*

26) Boston: Biographical Review Publishing Company. *Biographical Review; This volume contains biographical sketches of leading citizens of Livingston and Wyoming Counties, New York.*

27) Todd, Nancy L. *Historic and Architectural Resources of the Village of Mount Morris, Nomination Document.*

28) Begole, Josiah. *Pioneer Life: Genesee County.*

29) *Albany Argus*, Albany, NY. September 3, 1836, 3.

30) *War of 1812 Pension Application Files Index, 1812–1815.*

31) Ancestry.com. *History of Livingston County, New York: with illustrations and biographical sketches of some of its prominent men and pioneers* [database on-line]. (Provo, UT: Ancestry.com Operations Inc, 2005). Original data: Smith, James H. "George T. Ewart," *History of Livingston County, New York: with illustrations and biographical sketches of some of its prominent men and pioneers.* (Syracuse, NY: D. Mason, 1881), 107.

32) 1850 US Federal Census, Mount Morris, New York. Households #439 and #440.

## Chapter Three

33) *Sacramento Transcript*, Vol. 3, No. 6, 5. April 1, 1851.

34) Nevada County Chattel Mortgages, May 3, 1851, Book CM 3, p. 207. Nevada City, CA.

35) Brower, Maria. *Gold Rush Towns of Nevada County*, 13.

36) Comstock, David A. *Lives of Nevada County Pioneers.*

37) Ibid.

38) Brady, J. *You Bet Gold Fever.*

39) Red Dog Cemetery. usgwarchives.net/ca/nevada.cemeteries/reddog.txt. (accessed March 8, 2012).

40) Personal correspondence from David A. Comstock, September 1, 2016.

41) Comstock, David A. "The Man Who Rediscovered Red Dog."

42) *Sacramento Daily Union*, Vol. 10, No. 1443, November 9, 1855.

43) Comstock, David A., Ed. "News and Advertising in the Early Gold

Camps of Nevada County California (1850–1865)", "Nevada Journal, January 5, 1855", 1855.1. *CD-ROM*, (Santa Rosa, CA: Comstock Bonanza Press, 2016).

44) Ibid, 56.
45) Ibid, 60.
46) Comstock, David A., Ed. "March 21, 1861." *News and Advertising in the Early Gold Camps of Nevada County California (1850–1865)*.
47) Comstock, David A., Ed. Brides of the Gold Rush: The Nevada County Chronicles, 1851–1859, 211.
48) Comstock, David A., Ed. "March 21, 1861." *News and Advertising in the Early Gold Camps of Nevada County California (1850–1865)*.
49) Hutchings, James M. "Sheet Iron Penstocks for Hydraulic Mining." *Hutchings Illustrated California Magazine*, Vol. 1, July 1856 to June 1857, 520.
50) Mining in Nevada County: Red Dog Hill. *Sacramento Daily Union*. Vol. 13, No. 1891, April 18, 1857.
51) Election returns: Township Officers. *Sacramento Daily Union*, Vol. 13, No. 2015, September 10, 1857.
52) *Daily Democratic State Journal*, Sacramento, California. Vol. XII, Issue 35, p. 2. February 11, 1858.
53) 51 Bean, Edwin F. "Cement Mining," *Bean's History and Directory of Nevada County, California*, 58.
54) "Independent Convention in Nevada," *Sacramento Daily Union*, Vol. 15, No. 2295, August 5, 1858.
55) Bean, Edwin F. "Sketch of Little York Township," *Bean's History and Directory of Nevada County, California*, 367.
56) California Mines. *Sacramento Daily Union*. Vol. 16, No. 2425, January 4, 1859.
57) 55 Nevada County Chattel Mortgages, June 13, 1859, Book 3, 285; May 1, 1860, Book 4, 444. Nevada City, CA.
58) Nevada County Deeds, May 21, 1860, Book 6, 225–226. Nevada City, California.
59) Comstock, David A., Ed. "March 21, 1861." *News and Advertising in the Early Gold Camps of Nevada County California (1850–1865)*.

60) Bean, Edwin F. "Sketch of Little York Township". *Bean's History and Directory of Nevada County, California*, 371.
61) "Blue Lead Gold Mine." Claims for Sale, Advanced Geologic Exploration. Chester, California.
62) Bean, Edwin F. "Mines and Mining," *History and Directory of Nevada County*, 48-64.
63) Comstock, David A., Ed. "March 21, 1861." *News and Advertising in the Early Gold Camps of Nevada County California (1850–1865)*, March 1861, 99.
64) Ibid., March 7, 1862, Book 10, 331, and July 5, 1862, Book 10, 452.
65) "Fire at Little York." *Sacramento Daily Union*, Vol. 22, No. 3293, October 17, 1861.
66) "The Highest Water in 1862." *Sacramento Daily Union*. Vol. 24, No. 3683, January 10, 1862.
67) "Masonic Lodge in Red Dog."
68) *Daily Alta California*. Vol. 16, No. 5212, June 10, 1864, and Vol. 16, No. 5315, September 21, 1864.
69) *History of the Little York Union Guard*. Compiled by the Works Progress Administration (WPA) in Conjunction with the California National Guard and California State Library.
70) Starr, Kevin. *Americans and the California Dream: 1850–1915*.
71) *History of the Little York Union Guard*. Compiled by the Works Progress Administration (WPA) in Conjunction with the California National Guard and California State Library.
72) Comstock, David A., Ed. "March 21, 1861." *News and Advertising in the Early Gold Camps of Nevada County California (1850–1865)*. February 1, 1866, 78-79; 127.
73) Bean, Edwin F. "Sketch of Little York Township," *Bean's History and Director of Nevada County, California*, 371.
74) Wells, Harry L. *History of Nevada County, California; with Illustrations Descriptive of Its Scenery, Residences, Public Buildings, Fine Blocks and Manufactures*.
75) "Destructive Fire, Red Dog In Ashes." *San Francisco Bulletin*. August 18, 1866.

76) Bean, Edwin F. "Sketch of Little York Township Advertisements," *Bean's History and Directory of Nevada County, California*, 371.
77) "Masonic Lodge in Red Dog."
78) Bean, Edwin F. "Sketch of Little York Township Advertisements," *Bean's History and Directory of Nevada County, California*, 390.
79) Raymond, Rossiter W. *Statistics of Mines and Mining in the States and territories West of the Rocky Mountains*, 81–82
80) Brown, Juanita Kennedy. *Nuggets of Nevada County History*, 20.
81) Chatterjee, Pratap. "Legacy of Poison," *Gold, Greed and Genocide*.
82) Wells, Harry L. *History of Nevada County, California; with Illustrations Descriptive of Its Scenery, Residences, Public Buildings, Fine Blocks and Manufacturies*.
83) *Sacramento Daily Union*, Vol. 38, No. 5813.
84) Wells, Harry L. *History of Nevada County, California; with Illustrations Descriptive of Its Scenery, Residences, Public Buildings, Fine Blocks and Manufacturies* , 70
85) Brown, Juanita Kennedy. *Nuggets of Nevada County History*, 20.
86) Watkins, C. E. Boston Hydraulic Mine (Piping), Nevada County, California.

## Chapter Four

87) *San Diego Union*, September 18, 1878, p. 1.
88) MacPhail, Elizabeth C. *The Story of New San Diego and Its Founder Alonzo E. Horton*, 29.
89) Ibid., 56.
90) William Cleveland, a San Diego lawyer, Bank of San Diego founder, and co-owner with his brother David Cleveland of "Cleveland's Addition" and numerous other properties, had arrived in San Diego in 1865. S. W. Craigue was a prominent wine and liquor dealer, was elected County Sheriff in 1871, and later served as Chamber of Commerce president.
91) Bradt had arrived in San Diego a few months ahead of W. A. from an assortment of business adventures and a stint on the Republican-leaning 1856 Vigilance Committee in San Francisco. After only a few months as proprietor of the old San Diego

Hotel, Colonel Bradt sold out of the hotel business in favor of the real estate business. Bradt became the sole agent for subdivided properties in Manasse and Schiller's Addition also in New Town, adjacent on the east to Horton's Addition, and other very valuable and prominent properties. Before getting into the real estate business in the 1870s with their subdivision in New Town, Joseph Manasse and his partner Marcus Schiller had delved into a potpourri of enterprises since their arrival in town some fifteen years earlier, including hide brokering and lumber dealing. Like W. A. Begole, both Manasse and Schiller also served terms as San Diego City Trustees, Manasse being one of the three Trustees who helped expedite Horton's purchase.

92) *San Diego Union*, July 7, 1871, 4.
93) "J. Judson Ames" February 9, 2016.
94) Shiraishi, Sean K. T. Freemasonry in Old Town San Diego. California Department of Parks and Recreation.
95) Dunn, Theron. Masonic History of the Grand Lodge of California.
96) *San Diego Union*, September 6, 1901.
97) See bibliography for San Diego histories by Crawford, Engstrom, MacPhail, Pourade, Smythe, and Van Dyke.
98) MacPhail, Elizabeth C. *The Story of New San Diego and Its Founder Alonzo E. Horton*, 52.

# CHAPTER FIVE

99) MacPhail, Elizabeth C. *The Story of New San Diego and of Its Founder Alonzo E. Horton*, 53.
100) Pourade, Richard F. *The History of San Diego: The Glory Years*. Vol. 4, 141–152.
101) Engstrand, I. *San Diego: California's Cornerstone*, 96.
102) Gregg,E., Ed. "Appendix, Selected Chronological List of San Diego City Officials, Five-Member Board of Trustees, 1872—1889." *The Journal of San Diego History*.
103) Phillips, Iris. *The Railroad Story of San Diego County*.
104) C. D. Begole, one of the earliest white settlers of Lone Pine, was born in Sylvan, Michigan, in 1836 to W. A. Begole's first cousin,

another William Augustus Begole, and his wife, Abigail Nowland Begole. Around the same time, C. D. Begole's younger brother, prospector Augustus William Begole and his partner Jack Echols "discovered a swarm of rich silver bearing veins" in the mountains near present day Ouray. A. W. Begole eventually sold his stake, opened a grocery store in Ouray, and later moved to Denver, where he was joined by a niece and a nephew, George Davis Begole. George Davis Begole served as the mayor of Denver, 1931–1935. Whether these Begole relations scattered across the Colorado and California wilderness knew one another is unknown.

105) Fabert, Wayne M., and Ann Kantor. "San Diego's Centennial Celebration: A Pictorial Essay."
106) *San Diego Union.* September 18, 1878.
107) "San Diego Gaslamp Quarter Architecture and History Tour."
108) *San Diego Union*, May 9, 1878, p. 1.
109) *San Diego Union*, May 28, 1878, 1.
110) Whether Republican Arthur Julian and Democrat Jacob Julian were kin is likely, but unknown by the author.
111) "Another Lie Nailed: The Latest Grist of the Slander Mill Sifted." *San Diego Union.* August 28, 1875, 3.
112) San Francisco Bulletin, June 3, 1878, 1.
113) *Sacramento Daily Record-Union*, Vol. 2, No. 83, May 27, 1876.
114) *San Diego Union*, December 23, 1879, p. 4.
115) Smythe, William E. *History of San Diego, 1542–1908*, 391–412.
116) Pourade, Richard F. *The History of San Diego: The Glory Years*, Vol. 4, 160.
117) Occupational information compiled from San Diego City Directories and histories (See bibliography: Bynon 1886-7; Maxwell 1887-1888; Monteith 18889-1890; Olmstead 1895 and 1897; Thom 1893-1894; and MacPhail 1979; Pourade 1964, and Smythe,1907).
118) *San Diego Union.* April 26, 1881, 4, col 1.
119) Rickey Family Association Database, www. rickeyfamily.org (accessed March 23, 2016). "George White Butterfield" married Jessie Louise Rickey. Information provided by their daughter, Helen Butterfield Muehleisen of San Diego. (A connection to the Butter-

field Stage family is possible. There are hundreds of Butterfields, all descendants of Benjamin and Ann Butterfield who emigrated to the US in 1634. Adding credibility to the Rickey family recollections outlined in this database is the 1900 Federal Census, which lists three cousins with the surname "Baker" living in G. W. Butterfield's San Diego household. Butterfield Stage founder John W. Butterfield's wife was a Baker; her maiden name was Malinda Harriet Baker. These Baker cousins are possibly her kin.)

120) Department of Commerce and Labor, US Bureau of the Census. "California." *Special Reports, Marriage and Divorce 1867–1906*.
121) "More Railroad Material." *San Diego Union*, February 18, 1882.
122) "His Journey Ended: The Father of Senator Bowers Passes Away at His Son's Home." *San Diego Union*, December 7, 1889.
123) Real Estate Transactions. *San Diego Union*, December 30, 1886, 3, and April 3, 1885, 3.

## Chapter Six

124) *San Diego Union*, March 16, 1882, 3.
125) *San Diego Union*. September 28, 1882, 3.
126) "Bilks and Tumors: meeting of the Young Men's Republican Club," *The Sun*, September 13, 1882, 3.
127) "Joint Senatorial Delegates and County Central Committee," *The Sun*, September 27, 1882.
128) "Funeral of Captain Olds," *The Sun*, October 4, 1882.
129) "Election Matters," *The Sun*, October 18, 1882.
130) "Superior Court, McNealy Judge," *The Sun*, October 28, 1882, 3.
131) Weisburger, Bernard A. *The Dream Maker: William C. Durant Founder of General Motors*, 33, 80–116.
132) "The Union Acknowledges a Pleasant Call from Ex-Governor J.W. Begole," *San Diego Union*, February 11, 1886, 3.
133) Hoyt, Frederick G. "Marketing a Booming City in 1887," *The Journal of San Diego History*.
134) Ibid.
135) The three firms were: Hanbury and Garvey; Davis, Bivens, and Simmons; and Kaufman and Syford.

136) Shields, Wilmer B. "Thumbing Through San Diego's First Directories," *The Journal of San Diego History*, San Diego Historical Society Quarterly.
137) Pourade, Richard F. *The History of San Diego; The Glory Years*, Vol. 4, 174
138) Pourade, Richard F. *The History of San Diego; The Glory Years*, Vol. 4, 193. For more on the froth and flavor of these heady times in San Diego, read Pourade, Richard F. "A Boom Nobody Would Believe," Chapter 12 in *The History of San Diego: The Glory Years* and MacPhail, Elizabeth C., *The Big Boom 1886–1888, The Story of New San Diego and of Its Founder Alonzo E. Horton*. San Diego: San Diego Historical Society, 1979, 72–87.

## Chapter Seven

139) Pourade, Richard F. *The History of San Diego; The Glory Years*, Vol. 4, 159. Chapter XI is also a good summary of events.
140) "Murrieta Timeline," *About the City*. City of Murrieta, CA website.
141) Real Estate Transactions, *San Diego Union*. July 25, 1886, 3.
142) *California Great Registers, 1866–1910*, "W. A. Begole, 1886"; Voter Registration, Murietta, San Diego, California.
143) *San Diego Union Tribune*. May 2, 1886, 3 col. 3.
144) Bynon, A A. *San Diego City and County Directory*, 1886–1887.
145) "Gypsy Crime: Inquest on the Body of Lucco Marovich's Victim." *San Diego Union*, November 30, 1887, 5.
146) "Meeting of the City Trustees," *San Diego Union*, July 20, 1886, 3.
147) "Harrison and Morton; Enthusiastic Club Organized at Turner Hall," *San Diego Union*, August 17, 1888, 5.
148) "San Diego Judges for the November Election; the Wards and Precincts," *San Diego Union*, October 19, 1888, 1.
149) "A Small Vote: Fifteen Freeholders Who Will Make The Charter." *San Diego Union*, December 6, 1888, 1.
150) "Coronado Items," *San Diego Union*. December 8, 1888, 8.
151) Smythe, William E. Chapter II: Political Affairs and Municipal Campaigns, *History of San Diego*, 467–468

152) Monteith, John C. *Monteith's Directory of San Diego and Vicinity for 1889–1890.*
153) "In The Harness: The New Common Council is Duly Organized." *San Diego Weekly Union,* May 9, 1889, 8. This is a lengthy, detailed article that reveals much about San Diego's issues and leaders at the turn of this decade.
154) "In the Harness: The New Common Council is Duly Organized." *San Diego Weekly Union,* May 9, 1889, 8.
155) Ibid. Gunn's statement is well worth reading in its entirety.
156) MacPhail, Elizabeth C. *When the Red Lights Went Out in San Diego: Shady Ladies in the "Stingaree District"* (San Diego, California: San Diego Historical Society, 1974), 4.
157) Smythe, William E. *History of San Diego, 1542–1908,* 455.
158) "Douglas Gunn Dead: His Body Found Yesterday Afternoon in His Private Office." *San Diego Union.* November 29, 1891, 1.
159) Crawford, Richard. "San Diego Pioneer Moved from Newspapers to Mayor's Chair," *San Diego Union Tribune,* August 25, 2011.

# Chapter Eight

160) MacPhail, Elizabeth C. *The Story of New San Diego and Its Founder Alonzo E. Horton,* 109–128.
161) Olmstead Company, *Directory of San Diego City and County, 1897.*
162) "Local Intelligence." *San Diego Weekly Union,* July 11, 1893.
163) *San Diego Union,* November 15, 1894, 3.
164) "Mining News." *San Diego Evening Tribune,* May 4, 1896, 4.
165) Hennessey, Gregg R. "The Politics of Water in San Diego 1895–1897." *The Journal of San Diego History,* San Diego Historical Society Quarterly, Vol. 24, No. 3, Summer 1978.
166) *San Diego Evening Tribune,* October 5, 1897, 4.
167) *San Diego Union,* December 16, 1897, 8.
168) *San Diego Union,* October 13, 1898, 8.
169) "Knights Templar; Public Installation of New Officers Last Night," *San Diego Evening Tribune,* May 16, 1900, 5.
170) "Annual Meeting," *San Diego Evening Tribune,* March 4, 1900, 4.

171) The arrival of the Chandlers in San Diego sometime between 1880 and 1882 is inferred by their presence in Mendocino County (1880 US Census, viewed on Ancestry.com) and Henry L. Chandler's registration as a voter in San Diego (California, Voter Registers, San Diego, October 7, 1882, viewed on Ancestry.com), and by reference in Caroline's obituary to her "residence in this city for the past twenty years" ["Death of Mrs. Chandler," *San Diego Evening Tribune*, August 23, 1900. Digital images, GenealogyBank, http://genealogybank.com (accessed October 19, 2016) Historical Newspapers].
172) "Personal Notes," *San Diego Evening Tribune*, July 25, 1900.
173) *San Diego Union*, September 5, 1901.
174) *San Diego Union*, September 6, 1901.
175) *San Diego Union*, September 5, 1901.

# Bibliography

"A Small Vote: Fifteen Freeholders Who Will Make the Charter." *San Diego Union*, December 6, 1888, 1. Digital images, GenealogyBank. Accessed March 23, 2016 http://genealogybank.com, Historical Newspapers.

Advanced Geologic Exploration Company. Claims for Sale, Chester, California. Website, Retrieved March 18, 2012.

*Albany Argus*, Albany, NY. September 3, 1836, 3. Digital images, GenealogyBank. Accessed October 5, 2016 http://genealogybank.com, Historical Newspapers.

Ancestry.com. *History of Livingston County, New York: with illustrations and biographical sketches of some of its prominent men and pioneers* [database on-line]. (Provo, UT: Ancestry.com Operations Inc, 2005). Original data: Smith, James H. "George T. Ewart," *History of Livingston County, New York: with illustrations and biographical sketches of some of its prominent men and pioneers.* (Syracuse, NY: D. Mason, 1881), 107.

"Annual Meeting," *San Diego Evening Tribune*, March 4, 1900, 4. Digital images, GenealogyBank. Accessed March 23, 2016 http://genealogybank.com, Historical Newspapers.

"Another Lie Nailed: The Latest Grist of the Slander Mill Sifted." *San Diego Union*. August 28, 1875, 3 Digital images, GenealogyBank. Accessed March 23, 2016 http://genealogybank.com, Historical Newspapers.

Bean, Edwin F. *Bean's History and Directory of Nevada County, California*. Nevada: Daily Gazette Book and Job Office, 1858.

———. *Bean's History and Directory of Nevada County, California*. Nevada: Daily Gazette Book and Job Office, 1867.

———. "Cement Mining," *Bean's History and Directory of Nevada County, California*. Nevada: Daily Gazette Book and Job Office, 1858) 58.

———. "Mines and Mining," *History and Directory of Nevada County California*. Nevada: Daily Gazette Book and Job Office,1867), 48-64.

———. "Sketch of Little York Township," *Bean's History and Directory of Nevada County, California*. Nevada: Daily Gazette Book and Job Offcie,1867), 367.

Begole, A. W. Statement, October 9, 1886. *Pacific and Western Manuscripts*, Vol. 1. H. H. Bancroft Collection, The Bancroft Library, University of California, Berkeley, California.

Begole, Josiah. *Pioneer Life: Genesee County*. Address at the Pioneer Picnic held at Long Lake. August 24, 1882.

"Bilks and Tumors: Meeting of the Young Men's Republican Club," *The Sun*, September 13, 1882, 3. Digital images, GenealogyBank. Accessed March 23, 2016 http://genealogybank.com, Historical Newspapers.

Biographical Review Publishing Company. *Biographical Review: This Volume Contains Biographical Sketches of Leading Citizens of Livingston and Wyoming Counties*. New York and Boston: Biographical Review Publishing Company, 1895.

"Blue Lead Gold Mine." Claims for Sale, Advanced Geologic Exploration. Chester, California. Web. (accessed March 18, 2012).

Brady, Jerry. *You Bet Gold Fever*. San Pedro, CA: Golden Harbor Press, 1983.

Brandes, Ray, et al. *Gaslamp Quarter History*. Vol. 6, "Lots C&D North ½ East Side." San Diego: University of San Diego, 1976.

Brower, Maria. *Gold Rush Towns of Nevada County*. California: Arcadia Publishing. 2006.

Brown, Juanita Kennedy. *Nuggets of Nevada County History*. Nevada City: Nevada County Historical Society, 1983, 20.

Bynon, A.A. *San Diego City and County Directory, 1886–1887*. Los Angeles: Express Printing Company.

California Digital Newspaper Collection, Center for Bibliographic Studies and Research, University of California, Riverside. Accessed October 11, 2016 http://cdnc.ucr.edu

*California Great Registers, 1866–1910*, "W. A. Begole, 1886"; Voter Registration, Murietta, San Diego, California, United States, county clerk offices, California; FHL microfilm 977,094. Database, FamilySearch. Accessed March 23, 2016 https://familysearch.org/ark/61903/1:1:VT6F-6QT

California Mines. *Sacramento Daily Union*. Vol. 16, No. 2425, January 4, 1859. Digital images, GenealogyBank. Accessed March 23, 2016 http://genealogybank.com, Historical Newspapers.

Chatterjee, Pratap. "Legacy of Poison." *Gold, Greed and Genocide*. Chapter 8, Project Underground: January 1997. Web. (Retrieved April 25, 2016.)

Carrico, Susan, and Kathleen Flanagan. *San Diego's Gaslamp Quarter: Then and Now*. San Diego: Goodway Printing & Graphics,1989; Tecolote Publications, 2003.

City of Murrieta. "Murrieta Timeline." About the City. Accessed June 3, 2016 www.murrieta.org

Committee of Observation, Frederick County, Maryland. "Journal of the Committee of Observation of Frederick County, September 12, 1775–October 24, 1776." *Maryland Historical Magazine XI*. Baltimore, MD: Maryland Historical Society, 1916, 52.

Comstock, David A. Brides of the Gold Rush: The Nevada County Chronicles, 1851–1859. (Grass Valley, CA: Comstock-Bonanza Press, 1987), 211.

_____. "Lives of Nevada County Pioneers." CD-ROM, Version 1.2. Santa Rosa, CA: Comstock Bonanza Press, 2016.

_____. "The Man Who Rediscovered Red Dog." *Nevada County Historical Society Bulletin*, Vol. 64, No. 3, July 2010.

_____. "News and Advertising in the Early Gold Camps of Nevada County, California (1850–1869), compiled and edited by David A. Comstock." CD-ROM, Version 1.2. Santa Rosa, CA: Comstock Bonanza Press, 2016.

"Coronado Items," *San Diego Union*. December 8, 1888, 8, Digital images, GenealogyBank. Accessed March 23, 2016 http://genealogybank.com, Historical Newspapers.

Crawford, Richard. "San Diego Pioneer Moved from Newspapers to Mayor's Chair," *San Diego Union Tribune*, August 25, 2011. (Accessed March 23, 2016, from GenealogyBank, Historical Newspapers with the following search criteria: Name, W. Begole; Location, California; Date: 1840–1901).

———. *The Way We Were In San Diego*. Charlestown, SC: The History Press, 2011.

"Crossed the Plains with Donner Party," *San Francisco Call*, Vol. 87, No. 84, 3 September, 1901, California Digital Newspaper Collection, http://cdnc.ucr.edu/cgi-bin/cdnc, (Accessed March 17, 2012).

Daily Alta California, San Francisco, CA. *Daily Democratic State Journal*, Sacramento, *California*. Vol. XII, Issue 35. (Accessed March 23, 2016, from GenealogyBank, Historical Newspapers with the following search criteria: Name, W. Begole; Location, California; Date: 1840–1901).

*Daily Alta California*. Vol. 16, No. 5212, June 10, 1864, and Vol. 16, No. 5315, September 21, 1864. Digital images, GenealogyBank. Accessed March 23, 2016 http://genealogybank.com, Historical Newspapers.

*Daily Democratic State Journal*, Sacramento, California. Vol. XII, Issue 35, p. 2. February 11, 1858.

Department of Commerce and Labor, US Bureau of the Census. "California." *Special Reports, Marriage and Divorce 1867–1906, Part One, Summary, Laws, Foreign Statistics*. Washington, D.C.: Government Printing Office, 1909.

"Destructive Fire, Red Dog In Ashes." *San Francisco Bulletin*. August 18, 1866. Digital images, GenealogyBank. Accessed March 23, 2016 http://genealogybank.com, Historical Newspapers.

Devoto, Bernard. *The Year of Decision 1846*. New York: Little Brown, 1942.

"Douglas Gunn Dead: His Body Found Yesterday Afternoon in His Private Office." *San Diego Union*. November 29, 1891, 1. Digital images, GenealogyBank. Accessed March 23, 2016 http://genealogybank.com, Historical Newspapers. .

Dumpke, Glenn S. *The Boom of the Eighties in Southern California*. San Marino: Huntington Library, 1991.

Dunn, Theron. *Masonic History of the Grand Lodge of California*. Accessed May 24, 2016 http://beaconofmasoniclight.blogspot.com

"Election Matters," *The Sun*, October 18, 1882. Digital images, Genealogy-

Bank. Accessed March 23, 2016 http://genealogybank.com, Historical Newspapers.

Election returns: Township Officers. *Sacramento Daily Union*, Vol. 13, No. 2015, September 10, 1857. Digital images, GenealogyBank. Accessed March 23, 2016 http://genealogybank.com, Historical Newspapers.

Engstrand, Iris. *San Diego: California's Cornerstone*. San Diego: Sunbelt Publications, 2005, 96.

Fabert, Wayne M., and Ann Kantor. "San Diego's Centennial Celebration: A Pictorial Essay." *The Journal of San Diego History*, Vol. 22, No. 3, Summer 1976.

Family Search Database. "California Great Registers, 1866–1910." Accessed March 23, 2016 https://familysearch.org/ark/61903/1:1:VT6F-6QT (W. A. Begole, 1886; citing Voter Registration, Murietta, San Diego, California, United States, county clerk offices, California; FHL microfilm 977,094).

Faust, Laurel. "Tracing the Butterfield," *The Daily California*, September 1, 1991. (Accessed March 23, 2016, from GenealogyBank, Historical Newspapers with the following search criteria: Name, W. Begole; Location, California; Date 1840–1901).

"Fire at Little York." *Sacramento Daily Union*, Vol. 22, No. 3293, October 17, 1861. Digital images, GenealogyBank. Accessed March 23, 2016 http://genealogybank.com, Historical Newspapers.

First Census of the United States, 1790. Records of the Bureau of the Census, Record Group 29, National Archives, Washington, D.C. Viewed on Ancestry.com, and 1800 US Census, Conococheague, Washington, MD., Series M32, Roll 12, 152, image 160. Family History Library 193665, viewed at Ancstry.com.

"Funeral of Captain Olds," *The Sun*, October 4, 1882. Digital images, GenealogyBank. Accessed March 23, 2016 http://genealogybank.com, Historical Newspapers.

Geozone website. The Lost Oak Creek Mine: The Tale, 1. Accessed April 13, 2012 www.TheGeozone.com

Gunn, Douglas Maxwell. *Picturesque San Diego*. Chicago: Knight & Leonard Co, 1887.

"Gypsy Crime: Inquest on the Body of Lucco Marovich's Victim." *San

*Diego Union*, November 30, 1887, 5. Digital images, GenealogyBank. Accessed March 23, 2016 http://genealogybank.com, Historical Newspapers.

"Harrison and Morton; Enthusiastic Club Organized at Turner Hall," *San Diego Union*, August 17, 1888, 5. Digital images, GenealogyBank. Accessed March 23, 2016 http://genealogybank.com, Historical Newspapers.

Hendrickson, Nancy. *San Diego Then and Now*. London: Anova Books, 2003.

Hennessey, G. R., "The Politics of Water in San Diego 1895–1897." *The Journal of San Diego History*, San Diego Historical Society Quarterly, Vol. 24, No. 3, Summer 1978.

"The Highest Water in 1862." *Sacramento Daily Union*. Vol. 24, No. 3683, January 10, 1862. Digital images, GenealogyBank. Accessed March 23, 2016 http://genealogybank.com, Historical Newspapers.

"His Journey Ended: The Father of Senator Bowers Passes Away at His Son's Home." *San Diego Union*, December 7, 1889. Digital images, GenealogyBank. Accessed October 11, 2016 http://genealogybank.com, Historical Newspapers.

*History of the Little York Union Guard*. Compiled by the Works Progress Administration (WPA) in Conjunction with the California National Guard and California State Library. Digitized by the History Office, Camp San Luis Obispo, January 10, 2015.

Hoyt, Frederick G. "Marketing a Booming City in 1887." *The Journal of San Diego History*, Spring 1999, Vol. 45, No. 2, Ed. Richard W. Crawford.

Hutchings, James. M. *Hutchings Illustrated California Magazine*, Vol. 1, July 1856–June 1857.

Hutchings, James M. "Sheet Iron Penstocks for Hydraulic Mining." *Hutchings Illustrated California Magazine*, Vol. 1, July 1856 to June 1857, 520.

In The Harness: The New Common Council is Duly Organized." *San Diego Weekly Union*, May 9, 1889, 8. Digital images, GenealogyBank. Accessed March 23, 2016 http://genealogybank.com. Historical Newspapers

"Independent Convention in Nevada," *Sacramento Daily Union*, Vol. 15, No. 2295, August 5, 1858. Digital images, GenealogyBank. Accessed March 23, 2016 http://genealogybank.com, Historical Newspapers.

"Joint Senatorial Delegates and County Central Committee," *The Sun*, September 27, 1882. Digital images, GenealogyBank. Accessed March 23, 2016 http://genealogybank.com, Historical Newspapers.

"Journal of the Committee of Observation of Frederick County, September 12, 1775–October 24, 1776." *Maryland Historical Magazine XI*. (Baltimore, MD: Maryland Historical Society, 1916), 52.

"J. Judson Ames" February 9, 2016. Accessed May 23, 2016 http://www.sandiegohistory.org/online_resources/ames.html

"Knights Templar; Public Installation of New Officers Last Night," *San Diego Evening Tribune*, May 16, 1900, 5. Digital images, GenealogyBank. Accessed March 23, 2016 http://genealogybank.com, Historical Newspapers. .

Koschmann, A. H. and M. H Bergendahl. "Principal Gold-Producing Districts of the United States," Professional Paper 610. A Description of the Geology, Mining History, and Production of the Major Gold-Mining Districts in 21 States. US Department of the Interior. Washington, D.C.: US Government Printing Office, 1968.

Laurenz Wells, Harry. *History of Nevada County, California; with Illustrations Descriptive of Its Scenery, Residences, Public Buildings, Fine Blocks and Manufacturies*. (Oakland, California: Thompson and West, 1880).

Lewis Publishing Company. *An Illustrated History of Southern California*. Chicago: The Lewis Publishing Company, 1890.

"Little Slogan: Ownership of the Small Cannon Effectually Settled." *San Diego Union*, June 30, 1892, p.8; digital images, GeneaologyBank. Accessed March 23, 2016 http://genealogybank.com, Historical Newspapers.

"Local Intelligence." *San Diego Weekly Union*, July 11, 1893, Digital images, GenealogyBank. Accessed March 23, 2016 http://genealogybank.com, Historical Newspapers.

Lone Pine Pioneer Cemetery. Commemorative Plaque, Lone Pine, California.

Maxwell, George W. *Maxwell's Directory of San Diego City and County for 1887-1888*. San Diego: George W. Maxwell, 1887.

MacPhail, Elizabeth C. *The Story of New San Diego and Its Founder Alonzo E. Horton*. San Diego: San Diego Historical Society, 1979.

———. *When the Red Lights Went Out in San Diego*. San Diego: San Diego Historical Society, 1974.

"Masonic Lodge in Red Dog". n.p., n.d., Web. (Accessed June 16, 2010.)

McGrath, Maria Davies. "Augustus W. Begole," *The Real Pioneers of Colorado*, Vol. 1. Denver: The Denver Museum, 1934.

McGrew, Clarence Alan. *City of San Diego and San Diego County: The Birthplace of California*. Vols. 1 and 2. Chicago and New York: The American Historical Society, 1922.

McGuire, Bonnie Wayne. *Jerry Brady's Annual You Bet—Old Red Dog Tour*. Web, Retrieved April 24, 2016.

McMaster, Guy Humphrey. *History of the Settlement of Steuben County, New York, Including Notices of the Old Pioneer Settlers and Their Adventures*. Steuben County, NY: R. S. Underhill, 1858.

"Meeting of the City Trustees," *San Diego Union*, July 20, 1886, 3. Digital images, GenealogyBank. Accessed March 23, 2016 http://genealogybank.com, Historical Newspapers.

"Mining in Nevada County: Red Dog Hill." *Sacramento Daily Union*. Vol. 13, No. 1891, April 18, 1857. Digital images, GenealogyBank. Accessed March 23, 2016 http://genealogybank.com, Historical Newspapers.

"Mining News." *San Diego Evening Tribune*, May 4, 1896, 4. Digital images, GenealogyBank. Accessed March 23, 2016 http://genealogybank.com, Historical Newspapers.

Monteith, John C, Ed. *Monteith's Directory of San Diego and Vicinity for 1889–1890*. San Diego: John C. Monteith, Press of Gould, Hutton & Co. 1889.

"More Railroad Material," *San Diego Union*, February 18, 1882. Digital images, GenealogyBank. Accessed October 11, 2016 http://genealogybank.com, Historical Newspapers.

Morgan, Neil, and Tom Blair. *Yesterday's San Diego*. Miami, FL: E. A. Seaman, 1976.

"Murrieta Timeline," *About the City*. City of Murrieta, CA website. Accessed June 3, 2016 *www.murrieta.org*

National Aegis. "The Highest Mountains in the United States," October 8, 1873. Worcester, Massachusetts: Henry Rogers.

Nevada County Chattel Mortgages, Books 3 and 4. Nevada County Recorder, Nevada City, CA.

Nevada County Deeds, Books 6, 10, 14, 21, 26, 37 and 39. Nevada County Recorder, Nevada City, CA.

Olmstead, S.H. and A.A. Bynon. *Directory of San Diego City, Coronada and National City, 1892-1893*. San Diego: S.H. Olmstead and A.A. Bynon, 1892.

Olmstead Company, The. *Directory of San Diego City and County, 1895*. San Diego: The Olmstead Company, 1895.

———. *Directory of San Diego City and County, 1897*. San Diego: The Olmstead Company, 1897.

"Personal Notes," *San Diego Evening Tribune*, July 25, 1900. Digital images, GenealogyBank. Accessed March 23, 2016 http://genealogybank.com, Historical Newspapers.

Phillips, Irene. *The Railroad Story of San Diego County*. National City, California: South Bay Press, 1956.

Pourade, Richard F. *The History of San Diego: The Glory Years*, Vol. 4. San Diego: The Union Tribune Publishing Company, 1964.

Raymond, Rossiter W. *Statistics of Mines and Mining in the States and territories West of the Rocky Mountains*. Washington, D.C.: Government Printing Office, 1872, 81–82.

Real Estate Transactions. *San Diego Union*, December 30, 1886, 3, and April 3, 1885, 3. Digital images, GenealogyBank. Accessed October 11, 2016 http://genealogybank.com, Historical Newspapers

Real Estate Transactions, *San Diego Union*. July 25, 1886, 3. Digital images, GenealogyBank. Accessed March 23, 2016 http://genealogybank.com, Historical Newspapers.

Rickey Family Association, Rickey Database. <rickeyfamily.org> "George White Butterfield" (married Jessie Louise Rickey). Their daughter Helen Butterfield Muehleisen of San Diego provided the information.

*Sacramento Daily Record-Union.* (Accessed March 23, 2016, from GenealogyBank, Historical Newspapers with the following search criteria: Name, W. Begole; Location, California; Date 1840–1901).

*Sacramento Daily Record-Union,* Vol. 2, No. 83, May 27, 1876. Digital images, GenealogyBank. Accessed March 23, 2016 http://genealogybank.com, Historical Newspapers.

*Sacramento Daily Union.* (Accessed March 23, 2016, from GenealogyBank, Historical Newspapers with the following search criteria: Name, W. Begole; Location, California; Date 1840–1901).

*Sacramento Daily Union,* Vol. 10, No. 1443, November 9, 1855, p. 3 Advertisements. Digital images, GenealogyBank, http://genealogybank.com, (accessed 23 March 2016), Historical Newspapers.

*Sacramento Daily Union,* Vol. 38, No. 5813. Digital images, GenealogyBank. Accessed March 23, 2016 http://genealogybank.com, Historical Newspapers.

*Sacramento Transcript,* Vol. 3, No. 6, 5. April 1, 1851. Digital images, GenealogyBank. Accessed March 23, 2016 http://genealogybank.com, Historical Newspapers.

San Diego County Deed Books, 1846-1876, 1876-1885. San Diego County Assessor, San Diego, CA.

San Diego County Grantee Records, 1846-1876, 1876-1885, 1889-1891. San Diego County Assessor, San Diego, CA.

San Diego County Grantor Records 1876-1885, 1896-1899. San Diego County Assessor, San Diego, CA.

"San Diego Judges for the November Election; the Wards and Precincts," *San Diego Union,* October 19, 1888, 1. Digital images, GenealogyBank (http://genealogybank.com: accessed 23 March 2016), Historical Newspapers.

*San Diego Sun.* (Accessed March 23, 2016, from GenealogyBank, Historical Newspapers with the following search criteria: Name, W. Begole; Location, California; Date, 1840–1901).

*San Diego Evening Tribune.* (Accessed March 23, 2016, from GenealogyBank, Historical Newspapers with the following search criteria: Name, W. Begole; Location, California; Date 1840–1901).

*San Diego Evening Tribune,* October 5, 1897, 4. Digital images, GenealogyBank. Accessed March 23, 2016 http://genealogybank.com, Historical Newspapers. .

"San Diego Gaslamp Quarter Architecture and History Tour." GeoTourist website. www.Geotourist.com

*San Diego Union*, July 7, 1871, 4. Digital images, GenealogyBank. Accessed March 23, 2016 http://genealogybank.com, Historical Newspapers.

*San Diego Union*, May 9, 1878, p. 1. Digital images, GenealogyBank. Accessed March 23, 2016 http://genealogybank.com, Historical Newspapers.

*San Diego Union*, September 18, 1878, p. 1. Digital images, GenealogyBank. Accessed March 23, 2016 http://genealogybank.com, Historical Newspapers.

*San Diego Union*, December 23, 1879, p. 4. Digital images, GenealogyBank. Accessed March 23, 2016 http://genealogybank.com, Historical Newspapers.

*San Diego Union*. April 26, 1881, 4, col 1. Digital images, GenealogyBank. Accessed March 23, 2016 http://genealogybank.com, Historical Newspapers.

*San Diego Union*, March 16, 1882, 3. Digital images, GenealogyBank. Accessed March 23, 2016 http://genealogybank.com, Historical Newspapers.

*San Diego Union*. September 28, 1882, 3. Digital images, GenealogyBank. Accessed March 23, 2016 http://genealogybank.com, Historical Newspapers.

*San Diego Union Tribune*. May 2, 1886, 3 col.3. Digital images, GenealogyBank. Accessed March 23, 2016 http://genealogybank.com, Historical Newspapers. .

*San Diego Union*, November 15, 1894, 3. Digital images, GenealogyBank. Accessed March 23, 2016 http://genealogybank.com, Historical Newspapers.

*San Diego Union*, December 16, 1897, 8. Digital images, GenealogyBank. Accessed March 23, 2016 http://genealogybank.com, Historical Newspapers.

*San Diego Union*, October 13, 1898, 8. Digital images, GenealogyBank.

Accessed March 23, 2016 http://genealogybank.com, Historical Newspapers.

*San Diego Union*, September 5, 1901. Digital images, GenealogyBank. Accessed March 23, 2016 http://genealogybank.com, Historical Newspapers.

*San Diego Union*, September 6, 1901. Digital images, GenealogyBank. Accessed March 23, 2016 http://genealogybank.com, Historical Newspapers.

*San Diego Union*. (Accessed March 23, 2016, from GenealogyBank, Historical Newspapers with the following search criteria: Name, W. Begole; Location, California; Date 1840–1901).

*San Diego Weekly Union*. (Accessed March 23, 2016, from GenealogyBank, Historical Newspapers with the following search criteria: Name, W. Begole; Location, California; Date 1840–1901).

*San Francisco Bulletin*, June 3, 1878, 1. Digital images, GenealogyBank. Accessed March 23, 2016 http://genealogybank.com, Historical Newspapers.

*San Francisco Bulletin*. (Accessed March 23, 2016, from GenealogyBank, Historical Newspapers with the following search criteria: Name, W. Begole; Location, California; Date 1840–1901).

*San Francisco Call*. California Digital Newspaper Collection, Center for Bibliographic Studies and Research, University of California, Riverside. http://cdnc.ucr.edu with the following search criteria: Name W. Begole; Location, California; Date 1840-1901).

*San Francisco Call*, Vol. 87, No. 94, September 3, 1901. (Accessed October 11, 2016). California Digital Newspaper Collection, Center for Bibliographic Studies and Research, University of California, Riverside.

Sargent, Aaron Augustus. "A Sketch of Nevada County," in *150 Years Ago 1841–1851*. Arranged, illustrated, annotated, and copyrighted by David Allen Comstock. Nevada City: Nevada County Sesquicentennial, 1998.

Shields, Wilmer B. "Thumbing Through San Diego's First Directories," *The Journal of San Diego History*, San Diego Historical Society Quarterly, Vol. 2, No. 4, October 1956.

Shiraishi, Sean K. T. Freemasonry in Old Town San Diego. California Department of Parks and Recreation. Accessed June 23, 2016 http://www.parks.ca.gov/?page_id=25958

Smith, James H. *History of Livingston County, New York: With Illustrations and Biographical Sketches of Some of Its Prominent Men and Pioneers.* Syracuse, NY: D. Mason, 1881.

Smith, James H. and Cale, Hume H. *History of Livingston County, New York, with Illustrations and Biographical Sketches, Some of Its Prominent Men and Pioneers.* (Syracuse, NY: D. Mason and Company, 1881), 283–302.

Smythe, William Ellsworth. Chapter II: Political Affairs and Municipal Campaigns, *History of San Diego*, 467–468

——— . *History of San Diego, 1542–1908.* Vols. 1 and 2. San Diego: History Co., 1907.

Starr, Kevin. *Americans and the California Dream: 1850–1915.* New York: Oxford University Press, 1973.

Stewart, George R. *The California Trail.* Lincoln: University of Nebraska Press,1962, 301.

Steigler, Ione, Stephen Van Wormer, and Susan Walter. *Uptown Historic Context and Oral History Report.* San Diego: City of San Diego Planning Department. November 24, 2003.

Strauss, William, and Neil Howe. *Generations: The History of America's Future, 1584–2069.* New York: William Morrow, 1992, 206–227.

"Superior Court, McNealy Judge," *The Sun*, October 28, 1882, 3. Digital images, GenealogyBank. Accessed March 23, 2016 http://genealogybank.com, Historical Newspapers.

Thom, John. *Directory of San Diego City and County for 1893-1894.* San Diego: John Thom, 1893.

Todd, Nancy L. "Historic and Architectural Resources of the Village of Mount Morris," Nomination Document. Washington, D.C.: National Park Service, 1995.

Turner, Orasmus. *History of the Pioneer Settlement of Phelps and Gorham's Purchases and Morris Reserve.* Rochester, NY: William Alling, 1852.

"The Union Acknowledges a Pleasant Call from Ex-Governor J.W. Begole", *San Diego Union*, February 11, 1886, 3. Digital images, Genealogy-

Bank. Accessed March 23, 2016 http://genealogybank.com, Historical Newspapers.

US Department of the Interior. Geological Survey Professional Paper 610. "A Description of the Geology, Mining History, and Production of the Major Gold-Mining Districts in 21 States." Washington, D.C.: US Government Printing Office, 1968.

US Federal Census, Mount Morris, New York. Households, 1850, #439 and #440.

US GenWeb Archives, *Red Dog Cemetery.* http://files.usgwarchives.net/ca/nevada/cemeteries/ reddog.txt

Van Dyke, Theodore Strong, and T. T. Leberthon. *The City and County of San Diego; Illustrated and Containing Biographical Sketches of Prominent Men and Pioneers.* San Diego: Leberthon & Taylor, 1888. Reprinted Whitefish, MT: Kessinger Legacy Reprints, no date.

Watkins, C. E. Boston Hydraulic Mine (Piping), Nevada County, California. Number 1431, Hearst Mining Collection, Views by C. E. Watkins, California Heritage Collection, U.C. Berkeley, Bancroft Library

Weisburger, Bernard A. *The Dream Maker: William C. Durant Founder of General Motors.* (Boston: Little Brown, 1979), 33, 80–116.

Wells, Harry L. *History of Nevada County, California; with Illustrations Descriptive of Its Scenery, Residences, Public Buildings, Fine Blocks and Manufacturies.* Oakland: Thompson and West, 1880.

# INDEX

## ⁌ A
Adolph, John J., 18
American Party, 17
Ames, John Judson, 29–30
Ancestry (website), xvii
*S.S. Ancon* (steamship), 51
Ann Arbor, Michigan, 12
Aspinwall, Panama, 19
Avon, New York, 8

## ⁌ B
Baker, Malinda Harriet, 83
Balboa Park, 38
Barnes, George, 39
*Bean's History and Directory of Nevada County* (1867), 18–23
Begole, Abigail Nowland (in-law), 82
Begole, Augustus William (cousin), 75
Begole, Benjamin Bradley (brother), 7, 9, 11–12
Begole, Benjamin Franklin (father), 7–11, 76
Begole, Charles Dorrance (cousin), 40, 75, 81–82
Begole, Charles Myron (cousin), 53, 75
Begole, Cornelia Jane (cousin), 9
Begole, Eleanor Bowles (aunt), 8–9
Begole, Elizabeth (sister), 7, 9, 11
Begole, Frederick Augustus (cousin), 9, 11
Begole, Frederick Hurlburt (cousin), 76
Begole, George Davis (cousin), 75, 82
Begole, George William (cousin), 9
Begole, Joseph (brother), 7, 9, 11
Begole, Joshua (brother), 7, 9, 11, 67

Begole, Josiah William (cousin), xxiii, 9–12, 52–54, 75
Begole, Julia (cousin), 9
Begole, Margaret Schull (mother), 7–11
Begole, Mathilde (cousin), 11
Begole, Myron H. (cousin), 9
Begole, Nancy (sister), 7, 9, 11
Begole, Philo M. (cousin), 9, 76
Begole, Robert "Bob" (cousin), xviii
Begole, Sarah Eleanor (cousin), 9
Begole, Thomas Benjamin (cousin), 9
Begole, Thomas Jefferson (grandfather), 7
Begole, William Augustus
    during 1820s-40s, 4–5, 7–12
    during 1850s, 13–19
    during 1860s, 19-28
    during 1870s, 27–47
    during 1880s, 46-64
    during 1890s, 65–71
    as Alderman, 61–64
    arrival in San Diego, 1, 27–29
    birth of, 7
    business dealings of, 16–23, 33–35
    in California, xix
    City Charter and, 59–64
    as City Trustee, 40
    in Civil War, 21
    death of, 68
    defeat in election, 41, 44–46
    divorce of, 47–50
    family background, 7–12
    family story, xviii–xix
    funeral of, 33, 68–70
    gravestone of, 70
    as Justice of the Peace, 18
    leaving New York, 4

"life shift," 57–58
"Little Slogan" and, vii
in Little York Township, xvii, xxi, 4, 16–18, 20–21, 23, 41
marriage of, 47–50
Masonic activities of, 29–33, 66–69
mining activities of, 3–4, 13–23, 66–69
in Nevada County, xvii, xxi, 3–4, 13–28
obituary of, xxiii, 68–69
office at 529 Fifth Street, 3, 25, 28, 40–42, 60, 65–66
overview, 1–5
photograph of, ix
property in San Diego, 1–3, 27–29, 65–66
public service of, 33–36, 65–69
in Red Dog, xvii, 16–23, 41, 58
in Republican Party, 17–18, 27–28, 41–47
as tinsmith, 1–4, 15–17, 23, 32, 42, 58
Begole, William Augustus (cousin), 81–82
Begole, William Augustus (uncle), 8–9
Begole, William Franklin (cousin), 9
Begole, William Rivers (grandfather), 7
Begole & Company, Red Dog, California, 18
Begole Archeological Center, xviii
Begole-Higgins block, 41–43
Berry, John R., 60
Bills, Nathan, 11
Blue Lead Gold Mine, 18–20
Boston Hydraulic Gold Mine, 25
Bowers, James Marion, 49
Bowers, Lucy Horton, 49
Bowers, William Wallace, 27–28, 31, 34–35, 49–50, 52–54, 60, 69
Bowles, Thomas Augustus, 8
Bradt, G.G., 29, 31, 47, 66, 80–81
Brinkerhoff, Hezekiah, 9
Brown, Juanita, 25
Buick Motor Company, 53

Burgess, E.E., 47
Burlingame, Kansas, 67
Burroughs, D., 47
Bushyhead, Ed W., 27–28, 31, 52, 59, 66, 69
Butterfield, Ann, 83
Butterfield, Benjamin, 83
Butterfield, George White, 48, 83
Butterfield, John W., 48, 83
Butterfield Stage, 48, 83

## C

"C.A.," 54–55
Cajon Pass, 57
Calaveras County, California, 13
California Assembly, 35
California Militia/National Guard, 21
California National Bank, 65
California Senate, 52
California Southern Railroad, 47, 49
Camp Kibbe, 21
Campo gunfight, 34–35
Capron, John G., 47
Cassidy, Andrew, 45
Cave, Daniel, 31, 47, 59
"Centennial Gun," vii, 40
Chalk Bluff (town), xvii, 14, 17–18
Chandler, Caroline S., 67–68, 86
Chandler, Henry L., 67–68, 86
Chevrolet Motor Company, 53
Chicago, Illinois, 12
Christian, H.T., 62
Citizens and Commercial Savings Bank, 52
Citizens Non-Partisan Ticket, 60
Citizens Railroad Committee, xxi, 35
Civil War, 18, 21

Cleveland, Daniel, 27, 39, 80
Cleveland, William H., 27, 29–31, 80
Cleveland's Addition, 80
Colton, California, 47, 57
Commercial Bank, 39
Comstock, David A., 15, 17
Conklin, N.H., 59
"Copperheads," 28
Craigue, Solomon William, 29–31, 66–67, 80
Crane, D.A., 17
Crawford, Richard, 33, 64
Crocker, Charles, 46
Crosthwaite, Philip, 31
Culverwell's Wharf, 1

## D

*Daily Alta California*, 21
Dall's Saloon, 21
Dana, Charles Henry, 11
Dansville, New York, 8
Darnell, Thomas, 31
Davis, Bivens, and Simmons (firm), 83
Davis, William Heath, 29–30
Democratic Party, 18, 28, 45, 60
Denver, Colorado, 82
Derby, George, 31
DeVoto, Bernard, 5
"Discontented Seventies," 37–39
Dodge, Reverend, 48
Donner Party, xxiii, 4, 13
Donner-Reed prairie crossing, xxiii, 4
Double Standard Mine, 66
Dumke, Glenn S., 54
Durango, Mexico, 21
*Dutch Flat Weekly Enquirer*, 23

## E

Earp, Wyatt, 65
Echols, Jack, 82
El Cajon, California, 64
Engstrand, Iris, 33
Escondido, California, 67
Ewart, Harvey, 11
Ewart, Maria, 11, 76

## F

"Fair Play" letter, 41, 44
Fallbrook, California, 57
"Fannie" (dog), 46
Felsenheld, David, 46
Ferrell, William, 31
Fireman's Ball, 35, 39
Fisher (Alderman), 61
Flint, Michigan, 12, 52–53
Flint Wagon Works, 52–53
Flint Water and Gas Works, 52
Florence Hotel, xxii, 53
Fold 3 (website), xvii
Fort Yuma Road Company, 29
Frederick County, Maryland, 7
Free Coinage Mine, 66
Freemasonry
    Grand Lodge of California, 31–32
    Masonic Lodge No. 35 F&AM, xviii, xxii, 29–35, 38–39, 44, 52, 58, 67–69
    Mount Carmel Masonic Lodge No. 155, xxi, 20, 23–24, 30
    Nevada Royal Arch Masons No. 6, 25
    "Officers' Jewels," 32
    Royal Arch Masons No. 61, xxii, 25, 32, 52, 58, 67
    York Rite Commandery No. 25 Knights Templar, xxii, 32–33, 67
Fremont, John C., 4

French Huguenots, 7
Fuller, George, 67

## G

"Gallaghers," 60
Gaslamp Quarter, 41–42
GenealogyBank, xvii, xix
*Generations: The History of America's Future, 1584-2069* (Strauss & Howe), 5
Genesee County, New York, 7, 12
Genesee Valley, xviii, 4, 7–8
Geneseo, New York, 8
GeoTourist (website), 41
Gerwitz, Ellen, xviii
"Gilded Age," 65
"Gilded Generation," 5
Grand Lodge of California, 31–32
Grant, Ulysses, 35
Grant-Wilson Club, xxi, 35
Groveland, New York, 7–8, 11
Guadalupe de Los Angeles Gold and Silver Mining Company, 21
Gunn, Anna Lee, 39, 64
Gunn, Chester, 64
Gunn, Douglas, xxi, 27–28, 31, 34–35, 39, 48, 51, 59–65
Gunn, Lewis C., 27, 39, 46, 48, 64

## H

Hackett, Samuel Warren, 27, 31, 69
Hagerstown, Maryland, 7–8
Hanbury and Garvey (firm), 83
Hanford, Helen E. (wife), 39, 48–51, 57
Haraszthy, Agostin, 31
Harbison, J.S., 47, 66
Harrison, Benjamin, 58
Hawaiian Hotel, 41

Hawkes, D.F., 66
Hawkes, E., 66
Hayes, J.C., 47
Hazzard, George, 59
Heath, J.A., 66
Heydlauff, J., 22
Higgins-Begole Building, 41
*History of San Diego* (Pourade), xvii, 34
Hopkins, Mark, 46
Horton, Alonzo E., 1, 3, 31, 34–35, 37, 41, 49, 53–54, 60
Horton House, vii, 35
Horton Plaza, vii, 40
Horton's Addition, 1, 48
Horton's Hall, 39
Horton's Wharf, 1
Hotchkiss, A.B., 46
Hotel Del Coronado, 59, 64
Hotel Togo, 41
Houghton, J.F., 20
Howe, Neil, 5
Hoyt, Frederick G., 54
Hubbell, Charles, 47, 59
Hunsaker, W.J., 31
Huntington, Colis, 46
*Hutchings Illustrated*, 17–18

 **I**

Independent Convention, 18
*Inter Ocean* (Chicago), 54

 **J**

Johnson, A.H., 40
Johnson, E.B., 18–20
Julian, Arthur H., 41, 44–46, 52, 82
Julian, California, xxii, 3, 29, 45

Julian, Jacob M., 45, 82
Julian, Mike, 45

## K

Kaufman and Syford (firm), 83
Kimball, Frank, 46–47, 59
Klauber, Abraham, 31
Klauber, Allan, 34
"Know Nothing" Party, 17
Kurtz, Daniel, 31

## L

Lake Elsinore, California, 57
Langston, William, 17
Lee, Ole N., 1
Leicester, New York, 10
Levet, J.B., 41
Levi, Simon, 27, 31, 45, 61–62, 69
Lincoln, Abraham, 18
"Little Slogan," vii, 40
Little York Township, California
    business ventures in, 16–18
    fires in, 20
    mining in, 14
Little York Union Guard, 21
Livingston County, New York, 12
Lobdell, John, 17
Lone Pine, California, 40, 75, 81
Los Angeles, California, 21, 35, 40, 51
Low, Frederick, 21
Lucas, J., 40
Luce, M.A., 47, 59

## M

Mackie & Philip (bankers), 23

MacPhail, Elizabeth, 28, 33, 37, 65
Manasse, Joseph, 31, 81
Manasse and Schiller's Addition, 81
"Manifest destiny," 5
Marston, George W., 27–28, 39, 48–49, 60, 64
Maryland, xviii, 12
Maryland Company, 7
Masonic Building, 51, 67
Masonic Building Association, 51, 67
Masonic Lodge No. 35, xviii, xxii, 29–35, 38–39, 44, 52, 58, 67–69
Massachusetts, 48
McLachlen, Malcolm, 9
McNealy, Judge, 52, 67
Memphis, El Paso, and Pacific Railroad, 4
Mendocino County, California, 86
Mills, Hiram, 9
Mines
    Blue Lead Gold Mine, 18–20
    Boston Hydraulic Gold Mine, 25
    Double Standard Mine, 66
    Free Coinage Mine, 66
Monteith, John C., 60
*Monteith's Directory of San Diego and Vicinity for 1889-1890*, 60
Morgan, T.R., 17
Morris, Robert, 10
Morse, Ephraim W., 31, 34, 41, 45, 59
Morse, Philip, 51, 59
Morton, Levi, 58
Mountain Water Company, 66
Mount Carmel Masonic Lodge No. 155, xxi, 20, 23–24, 30
Mount Hope Cemetery, 33, 38, 68–69
Mount Morris, New York, 7–12, 53
Mount Whitney, 40, 75
Mule Ravine, California, 17
Municipal Ownership Club, xxii, 66

Murrieta, California, 57
Murrieta, J., 47

## N
Nash, H.C., 59
Nash, Joseph, 27
National and Commercial Bank, xxii
National City, California, 46–47, 57
Nevada City, California, 16, 25
Nevada County, California. *See also specific town*
    Cemetery District, 25
    Deeds and Chattel Mortgages, 18
    floods in, 16, 20
    mining in, 14
    W.A. Begole in, xvii, xxi, 3–4, 13–28
Nevada County Historical Society, xix
*Nevada County Transcript*, 22
*Nevada Journal*, 14, 16–17
Nevada Royal Arch Masons No. 6, 25
New York, New York, 19
*S.S. Northern Light* (steamship), 19

## O
Occidental Insurance Company, 22
Oceanside, California, 55, 57
"Officers' Jewels," 32
Old Nevadans Corresponding Committee, 46
Olds, Nelson, 52
Order of Red Men, 17
*S.S. Orizaba* (steamship), 51
Otay Valley, 47
Ouray, Colorado, 75, 82

## P
Pacific Insurance Company, 22

Pacific Railroad, xxi, 19
Pauley, Aaron, 27
Pauley, Frederick N., 31
Pendleton, George, 31
Perris, California, 57
*Picturesque San Diego* (Gunn), 64
Piley, Harry, 49
Pine Valley, California, xxii, 29, 66
Pourade, Richard, xvii, 33–34, 37, 55
Presbyterian Church, 48
Promontory Summit, Utah, 3

 Q

S.S. *Queen of the Pacific* (steamship), 51
Quirk, William, 20

 R

Railroads and railways
    California Southern Railroad, 47, 49
    Memphis, El Paso, and Pacific Railroad, 4
    Pacific Railroad, xxi, 19
    *The Railroad Story of San Diego,* 40
    San Diego, Cuyamaca, and Eastern Railway, 64
    San Diego Street Railway Company, 58
    Santa Fe Railroad, 67
    Southern Pacific Railroad, 40, 46
    Texas and Pacific Railroad, 35, 40, 44–45
Red Dog, California
    Blue Lead Gold Mine, 18–20
    Boston Hydraulic Gold Mine, 25
    business ventures in, 16–23
    Cemetery, 20, 25
    destruction of, 4, 24–25
    Fire Department, 19
    fires in, 20–23

  Haydlauff's Store, 22
  Masonic activities in, 30
  McGoun & Combs, 22
  mining in, 15
  Odd Fellows Hall, 24–25
  Pavilion Hotel, 22
  W.A. Begole in, xvii, 16–23, 41, 58
  Water Works, 20, 23
Reed, D.C., 66
Republican Party
  City Charter and, 59–60
  Republican Central Committee, 47, 52
  Republican Club, xxi, 58
  Republican County Committee, xxi, 35, 41, 45
  Republican County Conventions, 35, 45, 47, 52
  Republican National Convention (1872), 52
  Third Ward Republicans Presidential Election Committee, 58
  W.A. Begole in, 17–18, 27–28, 41–47
  Young Men's Republican Club, 52
Rickey, Jessie, 48
Robinson, James W., 31
Rochester, Nathaniel, 8
Rogers and Company, 18
Rose, Louis, 31
Royal Arch Masons No. 6, 25
Royal Arch Masons No. 61, xxii, 32, 52, 58, 67
Russell-Boggs wagon train, xxiii, 4

## S

*Sacramento Daily Record-Union*, 46
*Sacramento Daily Union*, 16, 20, 24
*Sacramento Transcript*, 13
*Sacramento Union*, 18, 20
St. Clair, Illinois, 12
Salvation Army, 41

San Bernardino, California, 52
San Diego, California
    during 1870s, 37–40
    during 1880s, 51–52
    during 1890s, 66–69
    arrival of W.A. Begole in, 1, 27–29
    Board of Aldermen, 59–64
    Board of Delegates, 59
    Board of Equalization, xxii
    "boom" during 1880s in, 51–52
    Chinese in, 37
    City Charter, xxi, 59–64
    City Trustee, W.A. Begole as, 40
    "Discontented Seventies" in, 37–39
    Fifth Street, 2, 59, 71
    Finance Committee, xxi
    Fire Department, 39
    Health and Morals Committee, xxi–xxii
    Native Americans in, 37
    "New Town," 1, 3–4, 27–29, 47, 57, 63, 81
    office of W.A. Begole at 529 Fifth Street, 3, 25, 28, 40–42, 60, 65–66
    Old Town, 1
    Police Committee, xxi
    property of W.A. Begole in, 1–3, 27–29, 65–66
    Public Buildings and Lighting Committee, xxi
    railroads in, 54–55
    Sewers and Health Committee, 63
    "Stingaree Row," 28, 41, 63
    Third Ward, 34, 41, 44–45, 58, 67
    University Heights, 64
    Water and Fire Committee, xxi, 66
San Diego, Cuyamaca, and Eastern Railway, 64
*San Diego Bulletin*, 29
San Diego Chamber of Commerce, xxi, 34, 39, 45, 54, 64

*San Diego City and County Directory (1897),* 65
*San Diego City Directory (1874),* 39
*San Diego City Directory (1886-1887),* 55, 58
*San Diego City Directory (1887-1888),* 55, 57
San Diego County, California
    Assessor, 66
    Board of Supervisors, 52, 58, 67
*San Diego Evening Tribune,* 68
San Diego Free Reading Room Association, xxi, 35, 39
San Diego Gaslamp Association, 41
San Diego Grave Groomers, 70
*San Diego Herald,* 29
San Diego History Center, xix, 29
San Diego Library, xxi, 35
San Diego Masonic Lodge No. 35 F&AM, xviii, xxii, 29–35, 38–39, 44, 52, 58, 67–69
*San Diego News,* 45
San Diego Railroad Committee, 46
San Diego River, 39
San Diego Royal Arch Masons No. 61, xxii, 25, 32, 52, 58, 67
San Diego Society of Natural History, xxi, 39, 46
San Diego Street Railway Company, 58
*San Diego Union,* vii, 27, 29, 33, 35, 40–42, 45–46, 67–68
*San Diego Weekly Union,* 61, 66
San Diego York Rite Commandery No. 25 Knights Templar, xxii, 32–33, 67
San Diego-Yuma Turnpike, xxi
San Francisco, California
    Great Fire (1906), 24
    Masonic activities in, 29–31
    railroads in, 40, 46–47
    San Diego compared, 55
    Vigilance Committee, 80
    W.A. Begole in, 1, 19, 35, 46, 51
*San Francisco Bulletin,* 22

*San Francisco Call*, xxiii
San Pasqual Valley, 48
Santa Clara Lodging House, 60, 65
Santa Fe Railroad, 67
Save Our Heritage Organization, vii, 40
Schiller, Marcus, 31, 81
Scott, Chalmers, 27, 31, 67
Scott, Thomas, 45
Sedgwick, Thomas, 4
*S.S. Senator* (steamship), 1
Shaffer, E.E., 67
Shields, Wilmer, 55
Simpson, J.H., 47
"Sixty-Niners," 27, 54, 63
Smith, Samuel F., 33, 69
Smythe, William Ellsworth, 33, 60, 64
*S.S. Sonora* (steamship), 19
Southern Pacific Railroad, 40, 46
Spreckles, John D., 64, 66–67
Stanford, Leland, 46, 59
Star Restaurant, 67–68
Steep Hollow Canal Company, 17
Stephens, A., 52
Stewart, William Wallace, 4, 27, 34, 52, 59, 67, 69
*The Story of San Diego and Its Founder Alonzo Horton* (MacPhail), 37
Strauss, William, 5
Sutter's Mill, 31
Swift, Colonel Philetus, 8

## T

Temecula, California, xxii, 57
Texas and Pacific Railroad, 35, 40, 44–45
Third Ward Republicans Presidential Election Committee, 58
Truckee, California, xxiii
Twain, Mark, 5

*Two Years Before the Mast* (Dana), 11

 V

Van Dyke, Theodore Strong, 33, 59
Vauclain, J.A.P., 66
Vermont, 48
Virginia, 7

 W

Walloupa (Waloupa), California, 16–17
Waloupa (chief), 17
War of 1812, 10
Watkins, Carleton E., 25
Watson, C.C., 47
Wayland, New York, 8
Wehmeh No. 1, 17
*Wells's History of Nevada County*, 21, 24–25
Westcott, Ed, 69
Wetmore, Charles A., 34–35
White, Lyle Lewis, 15
Wildy, Harry Hill, 34–35
Williams, W.L., 45–46
*The World*, 45

 Y

*The Year of Decision 1846* (DeVoto), 5
York Rite Commandery No. 25 Knights Templar, xxii, 32–33, 67
You Bet, California, xvii, 14–15, 19, 21, 24–25
Young, John, 41
Young Men's Republican Club, 52

 Z

Zink, Orion, 30

# Photograph, Illustration, and Map Credits

"Little Slogan," the 1876 Party Cannon.
  Courtesy David Marshall, A. I. A., San Diego, CA . . . . . . . *vii*
William Augustus Begole. Courtesy of San Diego Lodge
  No. 35 F. & A.M., San Diego, CA . . . . . . . . . . . *ix*
William Augustus Begole's Obituary. California Digital
  Newspaper Collection, Center for Bibliographic Studies
  and Research, University of California, Riverside,
  http://cdnc.ucr.edu . . . . . . . . . . . . . . . *xxiii*
Historical Sketch of the *S.S. Senator* at Horton's Wharf,
  *San Diego Journal of History*, San Diego History Center,
  San Diego, CA . . . . . . . . . . . . . . . . . *1*
Fifth Street Looking North from K Street, 1869–1870,
  San Diego History Center, San Diego, CA. Image 1659B . . . *2*
W. A. Begole's Tin Shop at 529 Fifth, 1874
  (Begole–Higgins Block). San Diego History
  Center, San Diego, CA. Image 10548 . . . . . . . . . . *2*
Ceremony of the Last Rail Spike. [Russell #223]
  Andrew J. Russell, May 10, 1869. Courtesy of the
  Gilder Lehrman Institute of American History,
  GLC04481.02 . . . . . . . . . . . . . . . . . *3*
Map of Nevada County Gold Mining Towns.
  Jerry Brady, San Pedro, CA. . . . . . . . . . . . . *14*
Map of the Historic Town of Red Dog,
  CA. David Comstock, Comstock-Bonanza Press,
  Santa Rosa, CA . . . . . . . . . . . . . . . . *15*
W. A. Begole's Advertisement in 1867 Bean's History and
  Directory of Nevada County, California: Containing
  a Complete History of the County. With Sketches of
  the Various Towns and Mining Camps, the Names and

Occupations of Residents; Also Full Statistics
of Mining and All Other Industrial Resources.
Archival image of page 390, supplied by
Internet Archive (at archive.org). . . . . . . . . . . 23
Boston Hydraulic Gold Mine, Red Dog, 1879.
Boston Hydraulic Mine (Piping) Hearst Mining Collection
of Views by C. E. Watkins. California Heritage Collection,
BANC PIC 1905 17175:111—ffALB. Courtesy of the
Bancroft Library, University of California, Berkeley, CA . . . . 25
W. A. Begole's Advertisement, *1870 San Diego Bulletin*.
Courtesy Newsbank Inc. . . . . . . . . . . . . . . 29
W. A. Begole's Application for Election to San Diego
Lodge No. 35. Author photograph. Courtesy San Diego
Lodge No. 35 F. & A.M. . . . . . . . . . . . . . . 30
W. A. Begole's handcrafted Masonic Officers' Jewels. Author
photograph. Courtesy San Diego Lodge No. 35 F. & A.M. . . . 32
Gaskill's Store in Campo, San Diego History Center,
San Diego CA. Image OP 1154. . . . . . . . . . . . . 34
W. A. Begole's Tin Trunk for San Diego Lodge Records. Author
photograph. Courtesy San Diego Lodge No. 35 F. & A.M. . . . 38
W. A. Begole's 1876 Invoice to San Diego Lodge
for the Tin Trunk. Author Photograph.
Courtesy San Diego Lodge No. 35 F. & A.M. . . . . . . . . . 39
W. A. Begole's Tin Shop at 529 Fifth Street, 1878.
San Diego History Center, San Diego, CA. Image 10965 . . . 42
W. A. Begole's Tin Shop at 529 Fifth Street, 2012.
Author Photograph . . . . . . . . . . . . . . . . 43
Masonic Building at Sixth and H Streets.
San Diego History Center, San Diego, CA. Image 1751-1 . . . . 51
W. W. Bowers' Florence Hotel. San Diego History Center,
San Diego, CA. Image 10965 . . . . . . . . . . . . . 53
First National Bank Building. San Diego History Center,
San Diego, CA. Image 1407 . . . . . . . . . . . . . 53
Fifth Street looking south from Broadway in 1888.
San Diego History Center, San Diego, CA. Image 792 . . . . 59

San Diego Lodge No. 35 Meeting Notice Advertisement,
    March 1900. Newsbank Inc. . . . . . . . . . . . . . . . . . 67
Mason's Notices in the *San Diego Union* of W. A.'s Death,
    1901. Newsbank Inc. . . . . . . . . . . . . . . . . . . . . 70
W. A. Begole's Gravestone, Mt. Hope Cemetery,
    Before and After 2016 Restoration. Courtesy of
    Thomas Patty, San Diego Grave Groomers, Escondido, CA. . . 70
Fifth Street, San Diego, Pictured Across Time.
    San Diego History Center, San Diego, CA.
    Images 1659B, 792, and 22463 . . . . . . . . . . . . . . . 71

# About the Author

The most thrilling moment of the author's five-year adventure researching and writing this story was the discovery of the 1876 tin trunk that W.A. Begole built for his beloved San Diego Masonic Lodge No. 35. Fashioned of heavy gauge tin sheeting, the 140-year-old treasure was likely put together between roofing jobs in Begole's tin shop at 529 Fifth Street in what is now San Diego's "Gaslamp District." The trunk was found in the Lodge storage basement, still stuffed with records that spanned W.A.'s life in San Diego, 1876–1901.

*Author Lael Montgomery with W.A. Begole's handiwork for which he charged the Lodge $3.50.*

Lael Montgomery is a North San Diego County activist and family history researcher who discovered several years ago, while reading Richard Pourade's multi-volume *History of San Diego*, that San Diego

"City Father" William Augustus Begole (1826–1901) is her first cousin, four times removed. While researching W. A. Begole's life and his place in her mother's family tree, she discovered that a cluster of W. A.'s nineteenth-century Begole kin, like him, also were intrepid, colorful, and notable settlers of the American West.

She holds an MEd from Harvard University Graduate School of Education and an MA and PhD from The Fielding Institute, all in cognitive and developmental psychology. She is mainly interested these days in discovering for herself and others how our family and personal stories fit into the story of America and how the journeys of ancestors we have never known leave traces in our own lives.

Lael lives in Valley Center, California, with her husband and a small menagerie of rescue cats and dogs, guinea hens, and heritage turkeys, all pets.

www.ingramcontent.com/pod-product-compliance
Lightning Source LLC
Chambersburg PA
CBHW040334300426
44113CB00021B/2751